HEART SOUL MIND STRENGTH

GODLY LIVING FOR TODAY'S KINGDOM CHRISTIAN

EVERETT LEADINGHAM, editor

Though this book is designed for group study, it is also intended for personal enjoyment and spiritual growth. A leader's guide is available from your local bookstore or your publisher.

BEACON HILL PRESS
OF KANSAS CITY

Editor
Everett Leadingham
Managing Editor
Charlie L. Yourdon
Senior Executive Editor
Merritt J. Nielson

Copyright 2006
Beacon Hill Press of Kansas City
Kansas City, Missouri

ISBN-13: 978-0-8341-2216-1
ISBN-10: 0-8341-2216-2
Printed in the United States of America

Cover Design
Chad A. Cherry
Interior Design
Sharon Page

10 9 8 7 6 5 4 3 2 1

Kingdom Christians are persons shaped by God's life until their most basic sense of identity, values, purpose, and place in the world reflect that citizenship. They love God with all their *HEART SOUL MIND STRENGTH*, and their neighbors as themselves.

CONTENTS

TRUTH TO REMEMBER

Kingdom Christians' treasures are in heaven.

TREASURES IN HEAVEN

BY JON JOHNSTON

Most of us take extreme measures to avoid pain and enhance pleasure. We cringe when hearing chalk screeching on chalkboards, eject bitter-tasting fruit, close our nose when encountering foul-smelling odors.

Conversely, we pay big bucks to hear favorite musical artists, treat ourselves to exotic coffees, and generously scent ourselves with fragrant perfumes. Indeed, we have a powerful natural inclination to embrace things that please our senses, but soundly reject that which yields the opposite.

Early Church martyrs undoubtedly desired fleshly comfort; but when it became "crunch time," they intentionally relinquished it for the higher good. Not because they were masochists. Rather, they shared a clear vision of heaven's glory and permanence, as well as our earthly sojourn's brevity. This is so clearly revealed in their final triumphant and inspiring words.

One saint, with arms and legs bound tightly with chains, victoriously proclaimed: "These aren't chains but ornaments. My feet may be fettered, but my soul still treads the path to heaven." As animal scrapers were being used to furrow the face of a young woman believer, she gazed heavenward and declared: "Lord, they are writing that Thou art mine." Another summed up his plight with this proclamation:

The world took my *citizenship,* but my (true) citizenship is (inscribed) in the Book of Life. The world (seized) my *possessions,* but I have treasures in heaven where no rust corrodes nor thieves steal. The world threatens to take my *life;* but if I am in the flesh, He is in me, and if I am out of the flesh, I'm with Him![1]

These, along with scores of their ilk through the centuries, shared a "this world is not my home" perspective. Like Abraham, they truly saw themselves as vagabonds here on earth, en route to a city having eternal foundations "whose builder and maker is God" (Hebrews 11:10, KJV). Bound for the Promised Land!

Contrast this with the 60ish woman I know, who faithfully devotes five hours each day in front of mirrors, taking drastic measures to enhance her appearance. Or the fellow who puts in enough work overtime, in attempting to guarantee his financial security, to qualify as both absentee husband and father.

Question: Which of these perspectives do we more tightly embrace? Is ours a holy, biblical, heavenly focus—with a loose attachment to mammon? Or, is our central focus on personal, sensual fulfillment and accumulation of resources in the here and now? As one poet poignantly asks: "Is this world too much with us?"

Is our gaze on, and obsession with, illusionary treasures on earth? Are we so thoroughly entangled in the "dense thicket" of the immediate and worldly to the neglect of the future and heavenly?

OUR VISE-GRIP ON THE TEMPORAL

To be candid, today there is a striking disinterest in heaven—certainly among unbelievers, but even among affluent North American Christians. In contrast to persons from more destitute places and times, most today have it so good that they rarely think about—much less yearn for—that "pearly white city" (Arthur F. Ingler, 1902).

God has showered the majority of people in our society with an abundance of earthly comforts—probably more than any prior generation. Furthermore, most know little of life-threatening persecution that has existed (and still exists) elsewhere.

Result: Few feel like strangers, pilgrims, or aliens in this world. More likely, many feel much like managers or stockholders. In lingo of the Old West, more like settlers than drifters. Roots are sunk deeply. Investments in the here and now are considerable.

Quite possibly, many would consider a summons to be with Jesus—at the indescribable home He has prepared—as a rather unwelcome intrusion into their busy schedule. A resented interruption of "important" appointments and "crucial" career goals.

With this in mind, it's little wonder so few write songs about "those golden shores" these days. The few hymns we sing about heaven are, mostly, spirituals or other oldies (e.g., "This World Is Not My Home," "When They Ring Those Golden Bells," "Swing Low, Sweet Chariot," "The Pearly White City"). Likewise, triumphant sermons on "glory land" —so plentiful in the past—seem very scarce today.

To many, indulging in excessive (or even minimal) "heaven-think" implies escapism, detachment with the present, being uselessly visionary.

TIME FOR A REALITY CHECK

Nevertheless, even today in our affluent, rushed, noisy lives, we who are twice-born must continuously remind ourselves that our truest homeland lies in the "land that is fairer than day, and by faith we can see it afar."[2] Heaven is spoken of no less than 582 times in 505 verses in God's Word. Our hearts should melt, and our hopes soar with inspiration and gratitude, when we read triumphant words like:

Our citizenship *is* in heaven. And we *eagerly await* a Savior from there, the Lord Jesus Christ, who, by the power that enables him to bring everything under his control, will transform our lowly bodies so that they will be like his glorious body (Philippians 3:20-21, emphasis added).

To lack this as our *dominant* focus is to ignore the obvious: In the grand scheme of things, life is extremely short. And compared to heaven, inconsequential—a brief and fleeting moment in time, in a place that is a "preparation zone" for our eternal home.

Concerning life's brevity, I recall gazing at the Great Wall of China as well as the Egyptian pyramids—both of which have stood in splendor for 3,000 long years—and thinking how brief my biblically allotted "fourscore and ten" years are by comparison.

Indeed, James hit the bull's-eye with these cryptic words: "What is your life? You are a mist that appears for a little while and then vanishes" (4:14). Many today accept that life is brief, but delude themselves into thinking they can be clever enough to slow down the hands of time.

In her book on heaven, Joni Eareckson Tada notes that the slogan, "Slow down and live," appears on everything from highway signs to health books. But time has a mind of its own, and we are helpless in attempting to decrease its velocity. Applying wrinkle cream, pumping brain and brawn with vitamins E and A, and even freezing the body in an iced hydrogen chamber (as did the late Walt Disney) won't do it. Steadily and consistently, time proceeds ahead, pulling us in tow.[3] As someone remarked: These hearts of ours beat like muffled drums—in steady cadence —as we march to our graves.

With this in mind, our attention must be fixed on life's "end game"—that which awaits us, our destination at the end of life's pathway. We must give primacy, as did the martyrs, to the eternal over the rapidly vanishing transitional and temporal. It only makes sense—especially for believers who possess an intense hope[4] and eager anticipation. Not only is this wise, it promises a multiplicity of bonus dividends in our earthly sojourn.

RESULTS OF AN AUTHENTIC HEAVEN-PERSPECTIVE

Granted, some have become so excessively heaven-focused that they're of little earthly good. Some mystics, for example, have intentionally isolated themselves from all semblances of earthly influences—as well as others' needs. Their goal? To deprive their flesh and, thereby, better contemplate the hereafter. Saint Simeon in the Middle Ages, for example, sat on a pole for 63 years, until his hair grew to the ground (and his back felt tortuous!). Few today share his mind-set. And that's probably not all bad.

But to repeat, today we're far more likely to err on the side of completely crowding out heaven from our conscious mind. And we do that to our detriment. Late scholar and admired friend, Bertha Munro, once drew a vivid contrast employing the ancient Greek myth of "Antaeus the Giant."

According to this legend, every time the big fellow was felled, he rose with new strength. Why? Because he had touched, and absorbed, vast amounts of energy from his mother—earth. But for us, the opposite holds true: contact with heaven, rather than earth, pours fresh strength into our spiritual veins.[5]

What are two very significant benefits resulting from an authentic heaven-focus dominating our perspective?

First, we clearly see how earth's treasures are deficient and, ultimately, unsatisfying—unworthy of our highest priorities.

Things, rather than God or people, can easily assume preeminence in our lives. The Bible refers to *mammon,* a Hebrew word for "material possessions." Originally it referred to entrustment to another for safekeeping, but it gradually came to imply "that in which a person puts his trust" (a god or God-substitute). No wonder Matthew 6:24 (KJV) proclaims that we "cannot serve God and mammon" simultaneously.

Grabbing, grasping, and putting trust in things is a favorite pastime today. Why? Affluence and advertising. The first provides means; the second supplies motivation related to defining our self-worth. Result: Throngs continually respond to their insatiable urge to satisfy fleshly desires. And gratification is rarely delayed! We combine our high maintenance with a very low threshold of patience.

Credit cards enable us to instantly own what we can't afford, go where we wouldn't be able to go, and do what would otherwise be impossible for us to do. Only later do we begin paying—for many only a minimum monthly total which mostly goes toward an exorbitant interest rate. Result? Endless debt. (Recently, I heard that the credit card debt owed by the average American family is $7,000—while, in contrast, the average savings account total is a paltry $3,000!)

Furthermore, the more we acquire, the more we desire —and desire to acquire. A deep-seated, insatiable urge seizes us, so that the very *act* of getting can actually become our most precious treasure. Little wonder that an increasing number of 12-step groups target shoppers' addictions.

In very graphic, no-nonsense language, our Lord tells us three reasons why such earthly treasures aren't worthy of our primary focus (see Matthew 6:19-21):

1. *Some are vulnerable to moth-consumption, hence, destruction.* The primary reference here is to clothes, no matter how costly or beautiful. The kind that Gehazi, Elisha's servant, connived to obtain from Naaman after his master had cured him (2 Kings 5:22). The kind that tempted Achan to sin when he set his affections on "a beautiful robe from Babylonia" (Joshua 7:21). At some point, all clothes hit the closet, and that's where little critters begin their feast.

2. *Many are prone to another kind of "eating away"*
   (Greek *brosis*) Only here in God's Word is it translated "rust." More likely, the reference is to rats,
   mice, worms, and other vermin invading granaries to
   consuming grain. So, to our clothes we can add this
   constant threat to our food supply.

3. *Finally, all valued earthly treasures are subject to being
   stolen by thieves who "dig through"* (Greek *diorussein*).
   In Palestine, walls of many houses were made of
   baked clay. Burglars easily dug through walls and
   seized all they desired.[6] Today, in spite of the highest-
   tech alarm systems, and the most vicious of guard
   dogs, thieves somehow succeed in invading our
   homes and departing with great quantities of "loot."

*Second, when we possess a "heaven-focus," our minds antici-
pate the incredible, completely satisfying, eternal treasures that
await us.*

When Jesus enters our hearts, our affections change.
Our attention is redirected away from degradable earthly
treasures, and toward incorruptible, incomparable heavenly
treasures, ones that never fade away. Some of these are:

1. *First and most important, our Father awaits there to
   welcome us.* Jesus taught us to pray, "Our Father
   which art in heaven" (Matthew 6:9, KJV). Furthermore, our blessed Savior is at His right hand, where
   He intercedes on our behalf (see Hebrews 7:25) and
   oversees the building of our palatial heavenly home
   (see John 14:2).

2. *Scores of our brothers and sisters in Christ are there* (see
   Hebrews 12:23). Joyce Landorf once referred to
   them as our "balcony people," who cheer us on to the
   finish line. Martyrs, biblical heroes, departed family,
   and friends will someday join us at the glorious, un-
   ending celebration that will make the one following
   the Super Bowl look like a child's tea party!

3. *Our names are indelibly inscribed there in the Lamb's*

Book of Life. Jesus once instructed His disciples, "re-
joice [because] your names are written in heaven"
(Luke 10:20). Why? Because that means we officially belong there.[7]

In addition to these, there are angels and unimaginable
surroundings: mansions for everyone, a crystal sea, gates of
pearl, walls of precious gems, and gold so plentiful that it's
used to pave roads! Beauty much too awesome to describe.

Furthermore, as Joni likes to say, "It's the land of the
'no-mores.'" They're listed in Revelation 21:4. No more sorrow, crying, pain, curse, and—praise be to God—no more
death. On earth, the sum of human misery vastly outweighs
that of human happiness. Job declared: "Man born of woman
is of few days and full of trouble" (14:1). David says: "Oh,
that I had the wings of a dove! I would fly away and be at
rest— . . . far from the tempest and storm" (Psalm 55:6, 8).

Bottom line: Heaven will be "an undoing of all the bad
things we know as God wipes away every tear and closes the
curtain on pain and disappointment."[8]

It all comes down to what Jesus proclaims: Everything
we love everlastingly, everything we rightly value, everything
of eternal worth is in heaven—pure and simple. That's why it
is worthy of our innermost thoughts and most exalted
dreams. Meanwhile, as the hymn aptly puts it, "The things of
earth will grow strangely dim"—as our hearts become galva-
nized on our glorious, eternal treasures (see Matthew 6:21).[9]

MORE MAGNETISM THAN MYSTERY

Since many associate heaven with the distant beyond,
our thoughts concerning it often lack intimacy. Result: Many
of us have little mental and psychological bonding with it, as
well as the idea of spending eternity there. But even though
it may seem far away and alien to our everyday existence, it
need not be dreaded nor relegated to a level of secondary

importance. To avoid this pitfall, we need only consider a couple of very important facts.

First, although many details about the great, mysterious beyond are unknown, some hints of its splendor are proclaimed in God's Word. We read of rainbow thrones, a 1,400-mile length and width, 200-foot walls made of jasper, mansions everywhere. But when all is said, the most important fact is that our Lord prepared it all. And His lavish love has never cut corners. With this in mind, C. S. Lewis summarizes:

All the things that have ever deeply possessed your soul have been but hints of [heaven]—tantalizing glimpses, promises never quite fulfilled, echoes that died away just as they caught your ear.[10]

They once asked NFL's Hollywood Henderson (Dallas Cowboys) on the eve of a Super Bowl whether he considered his upcoming experience to be the "absolute ultimate." He nonchalantly remarked, "Not really. You see, there's another one next year." By contrast, by all standards available to humankind, heaven will definitely be the absolute ultimate!

Second, although it may seem spatially and temporally distant, heaven is much closer than we think. Many religions maintain that after death, persons must travel distances, fight animals, endure great suffering, etc., before arriving in paradise. Egyptian belief, for example, posited that any departed Pharaoh must cross a river while waging battle with crocodiles. Not so with our faith. We know that our transition to heaven is an eye blink. It's just around life's corner, momentarily awaiting our earthly departure. To be absent from the body is to be present with the Lord (see 2 Corinthians 5:6-8).

And it is near. No land to trek, oceans to swim, nor mountains to climb. It is right then and there, just after our last breath is taken.

As Christians, although our intellect may accept these facts, there is often still a part of us that holds back—hoping that our earthly sojourn can, somehow, be extended. Much like what an unborn baby might say to his mother, while still in the womb. Imagine this *conversation:*

    Mother: "Do you realize that you are about to be born into a great big world full of mountains, rivers, and a sun and a moon?"

    Unborn: "No way. My best world is the one surrounding me—soft, warm, dark. I'll never be convinced that just a few hairbreadths outside this uterus exists this place you describe."[11]

There he is, safe in his little world, ignorant of the fact that a much more glorious world awaits him. A world for which he was created and is being fashioned. But only when he is actually birthed into it will he fully comprehend the truth.

Heaven has been pictured as an incredible party that begins for us the second we arrive. As our waiting time gets shorter, can we hear its increasing crescendo? The louder it gets in our hearts, the more willing we should be to relinquish our grasp on earthly life and its treasures.

Notes:

1. Taken from class notes in History of the Christian Church, taught by Mendel Taylor, 1964, Nazarene Theological Seminary.

2. Sanford F. Bennett, lyrics, and Joseph P. Webster, music, "Sweet By-and-By," *Worship in Song* (Kansas City: Lillenas Publishing Company, 1972), 255.

3. Joni Eareckson Tada, *Heaven: Your Real Home* (Grand Rapids: Zondervan Publishers, 1995), 100.

4. The biblical term for "hope" (Greek *elpis*) implies a solid expectation (e.g., our "hope" is in Christ, rather than some distant, vague notion that we might possibly anticipate—e.g., our "hope" that we receive a new sweater for Christmas).

5. Bertha Munro, *Truth for Today* (Kansas City: Nazarene Publishing House, n.d.), 326.

6. William Barclay, *The Daily Study Bible: The Gospel of Matthew*, vol. 1 (Philadelphia: The Westminster Press, 1958), 240-42.

7. John F. MacArthur, *The Glory of Heaven: The Truth About Heaven, Angels and Eternal Life* (Wheaton, Ill.: Crossway Books, 1996), 47ff.

8. Tada, *Heaven: Your Real Home*, 28-29.

9. Helen Howarth Lemmel, "Turn Your Eyes Upon Jesus," *Worship in Song* (Kansas City: Lillenas Publishing Company, 1995), 207.

10. C. S. Lewis quoted in article by Randy Becton, *Upreach*, vol. 10, No. 2, 7.

11. Tada, *Heaven: Your Real Home*, 80-81.

Scripture Cited: Joshua 7:21; 2 Kings 5:22; Job 14:1; Psalm 55:6, 8; Matthew 6:9, 19-21, 24; Luke 10:20; Philippians 3:20-21; Hebrews 11:10; James 4:14; Revelation 21:4

About the Author: Dr. Johnston is professor of sociology at Pepperdine University, Malibu, California.

TRUTH TO REMEMBER

Kingdom Christians are "born of water
and the Spirit."

SPIRITUALLY ALIVE

BY TIMOTHY B. PUSEY

Chet was a good man—generous, kind, easy to get along with, and always willing to help out at the church. There just weren't many people around more likable than ol' Chet! And throughout many years and the tenure of many pastors, he was consistently "the pastor's friend." Not only did Chet attend services, he even tithed! And yet, throughout the several decades of which I was aware, Chet never claimed to be a Christian. It was a mystery to everyone who knew him.

What makes someone a kingdom Christian? Is it about how we act and how we treat people? Yes, but there are a lot of nice people in the world who wouldn't claim to be Christians. Is it about service to others and working together with Christ's Church toward the accomplishment of Christ's mission in our world? Yes, and yet there are great humanitarians in the world and millions of people who have no comprehension of what it means to be a kingdom Christian and yet who are busily involved in churches and charities. And doesn't church attendance count for something? And certainly tithing has to earn some points with God, right?

A RADICAL TRANSFORMATION

Jesus had a conversation with an incredibly good man named Nicodemus one day. His credentials were impeccable

—a religious leader in the community. Nicodemus came to Jesus in the dark shadows of late evening. To the man's flowery greeting, Jesus responded on a completely different plane of thought, "I tell you the truth, no one can see the kingdom of God unless he is born again" (John 3:3).

Nicodemus must have laughed as he protested, wondering how an old man could go back into his mother's womb and be born again! But Jesus continued, "I tell you the truth, no one can enter the kingdom of God unless he is born of water and the Spirit . . . You should not be surprised at my saying, 'You must be born again'" (John 3:5, 7).

Jesus is saying that it's not enough to be a good, moral person. It's not enough to be a good humanitarian. It's not even enough to be consistent in coming to church or in tithing. We can only be part of the kingdom of God if we have been "born again." All the other things must come along in our devotion to God; but they aren't what make us Christians. We must have been made new within by the forgiveness and cleansing of Christ, who died so that our sins could be removed. And the Great News is that every person can experience this newness of soul. Every person can be made new in Christ. Every person can be born again.

To be kingdom Christians, we must experience a spiritual rebirth. Nicodemus was trying to be a kingdom believer without first being spiritually alive. He was still dead. He was living in darkness. He was missing the point, though he had learned how to go through all the right motions—just like ol' Chet.

As I write these words today, our family is rejoicing over the arrival of a new little great-niece into our extended family. Birth was the means by which Emily entered the world. Her life will never be as it was! It's a whole new world for her to explore—with all kinds of adjustments necessary, and yet she has somehow been divinely equipped to make all those adjustments to living in our world. It's all so exciting!

And *spiritual* birth is no less exciting and no less revolutionary! To be "born again" signifies a transformation of a person that is so radical that he or she is able to enter another "world" and a whole new way of living. Once again, Jesus has used a basic earthly reality to expound on a spiritual truth.

"A fresh start." "Starting new." "Another chance." The phrases are vibrant and energizing. Is it possible? Could this be what Jesus meant? Can our lives be so radically changed? I long ago concluded that the kind of transformation Christ has in mind for each of us is so radically powerful that the best phrase He could come up with to help us understand the depths of its meaning are the words "born again." As the apostle Paul wrote, "If anyone is in Christ, he is a new creation; the old has gone, the new has come!" (2 Corinthians 5:17). To be spiritually alive, we must be born again. And the best news is that we can be!

COMPLEX YET WONDERFULLY SIMPLE

But like many people today, Nicodemus obviously didn't understand what Jesus was saying. He was baffled and confused. This was not what he expected. In spite of all his religious training and his commitment to live by all the codes, Nicodemus was locked in his own flesh. He only saw from an earthly perspective. He couldn't see what God envisioned happening in his own life.

"No one can enter the kingdom of God unless he is born of water and the Spirit" (John 3:5). What is meant by the term "water"? Ezekiel 36:25ff. and Titus 3:5 speak of the washing of regeneration and the renewing of the Holy Spirit. To be born again is to be regenerated and also cleansed by the Spirit of God. And that's what entitles a person to enter the kingdom of God.

Let's be clear that this new birth is not just another attempt at trying hard to change ourselves with our best efforts. And it is not just a matter of continuing the status quo with, albeit, a few minor changes. It's not even just a concerted effort to obey all the ways of the Lord. No! We're talking "new birth" here—"the old has gone, the new has come." The old ways have had their day. A new day has come. And this new birth is by the Holy Spirit of God. The One by whose creative breath every person became a living soul also shares the life-transforming Spirit with all who will receive. This is the power from above that liberates and makes all things new.

Jesus told Nicodemus that the entrance into the kingdom of God could not be achieved by legalism or by outward conformity. When we truly become, by spiritual new birth, kingdom Christians, we are given new eyes and a new heart to grasp what it means to be a member of a new family. We are children of God! As His children, we are compelled from within to walk in step with this new family. As newly adopted children of the King, we respond with gratitude for all He has provided. And with this heart of gratitude, joyful obedience to the One who has done so much for us isn't such a stretch at all.

Nicodemus hadn't caught on to that yet. He had carefully studied the Law of Moses and was obviously striving to live by it all; but his legalistic approach was missing the heart of what God has for us. Ultimately, obedience to the laws of God is only accomplished in the context of fellowship with Him, and the door to such fellowship is the experience of being born again.

We use many different terms to understand this experience. The classic way to express this in the context of many churches in the past century has been to say, "I've been *saved*." We have come to God, seeking His forgiveness and the new life offered to us. Our lives have been *redeemed*— bought back by the shed blood of Jesus, who gave His life so that each one of us could be in fellowship with Him. We've been *adopted* into His family—claimed as His own with all the rights and privileges of natural-born children of the King. We've been *justified*—just as the convicted prisoner is pardoned of his crime and treated as if he had never done anything wrong at all. Some call it "regeneration"—which is simply another way to say "born again."

AN OPEN INVITATION

The New Testament is clear that membership in the kingdom of God is not the prerogative of any particular race or culture. That is why we must be careful not to force Christianity into the mold of our particular culture, but allow it to flourish for others in a culturally relevant manner. Scripture is also clear that membership in the kingdom of God is not hereditary. Someone long ago said, "God has no grandchildren." We do not become children of God by the experience of our parents, but each one of us must receive God's grace directly.

My wife and I have persistently desired that our three children come to love the Lord and to love His church. Attendance and participation in the life of our church was expected throughout their growing-up years. It was just how the people of our house were going to live. And it is certainly the responsibility of Christian parents to nurture their children in the ways of the Lord and to model before them what it means to be kingdom Christians. There is probably no greater responsibility that we have had as parents than this!

And yet, we have always been keenly aware that each of them must make his or her own way to God. We can encourage it. We can teach it. We can model it, but eventually they must make their own choice. I would never want to underestimate or minimize the influence of godly parents, and yet the whole goal of such is to help them find their way to the saving grace of God and experience what we have—being made "new creatures in Christ," born again.

In this way, our salvation experience is so very personal. That's why we must be careful not to press it into the mold of our own personal experience. For some, it is a tremendously emotional moment. For others, it is a quiet peace. For some, it ushers in radically observable changes in lifestyle, and for others this new birth begins a transformation that may appear to others as quite subtle but is indeed the turning point for a completely new approach to life. And just as Jesus spoke personally to Nicodemus, the gift of God's grace comes to each of us personally as well, meeting us right where we are and taking us on the unique journey of faith that our Creator God has designed for us to enjoy and experience.

A MYSTERIOUS YET POWERFUL LOVE

Still, it is not just another version of "the same old thing." The Church across the years has probably had far too many people living the same old way, just like Nicodemus—going through the motions quite well, but with no reality to the experience. They can repeat the right words and run in the right circles. They take on more projects and desperately try to act right. But at the center of their existence, in the deepest part of their soul, they remain untouched and unchanged. We have at times tried to whitewash the old, unchanged self—excusing it away or pretending it wasn't there. We may talk about all the things we do or all the money we give, but far too many are still empty and needy. The truth is that they are spiritually bankrupt, having never truly taken the step of total faith in Jesus Christ for salvation.

At verse 8, Jesus relates this experience to the movement of the wind. The wind can only be heard or observed in relation to its effect. In September 2005, the devastating effects of powerful wind were seen along the Gulf Coast of the United States as Hurricane Katrina left such devastation in her pathway. And despite the tremendous impact of those winds, you still couldn't have "seen" such wind. So it is with the wind of the Spirit of God in our lives. The origin and the destination of that wind are unknown to the one who feels it and acknowledges its reality. Nevertheless, the inability to see it with our eyes does not minimize the effects of the Spirit upon our lives, making us new creatures in Christ, truly born again. The breath of God brings life, not haphazardly, but according to His gracious purpose.

If you are reading these words and admittedly have never been born again, be assured that you can be! But you cannot come incognito like Nicodemus coming to Jesus late at night perhaps so that no one would know what he was pursuing. Our Creator God did not design us to live our lives apart from Him or in conflict with Him. He created us for fellowship with Him. He wants to come alongside us. He has provided for the forgiveness of our sins and the restoration of relationship with Him that becomes a tremendous joy and strength every day of our lives. Contrary to popular belief, He is not out to make our lives miserable and take all the joy out of living, but He does desire the best for us. God's best doesn't leave us wallowing in guilt from our past and does keep us from a lot of unnecessary heartache in the future.

Have you ever seen the placards held throughout the crowds at sports events, with just the biblical reference "John 3:16" on them? I suppose many of us know what that stands for, but it is incredible how many viewers today have absolutely no clue. As far as they know, a man named John is telling his friend what section to find him in—Section 316. But we know it as the reminder of a wonderful biblical truth —that God so loved the people of this world that He gave His only Son to die on a cross for us. The dialogue Jesus had with Nicodemus leads to one of the most well-known statements of the Bible, where Jesus declares to Nicodemus: "For God so loved the world that he gave his one and only Son, that whoever believes in him shall not perish but have eternal life" (John 3:16). Jesus was proclaiming to Nicodemus the wonderfully hopeful word of God's tremendous love for all people everywhere. And everyone who believes in Christ for salvation will not perish, but will have eternal and abundant life. Every person can be a kingdom Christian!

SUCH LOVE DEMANDS RESPONSE

What must you do to be born again? Acknowledge your sins to the Lord and ask Him to forgive you—and dare to believe that God will do what He says He'll do! Ask Him to help you live a godly life as you turn away from sin to follow Him. The wonderful promise is that God *will* make us new. He begins the process of changing us—cleansed from the inside out—and it all takes place in the context of a growing relationship with Him.

But not everyone knows about that, right? No, they really don't understand it. Many don't understand it because no one whom they trust has ever told them. They haven't heard a friend or a family member tell how Christ forgave their sins and accepted them into His family. One of the great privileges of kingdom Christians is sharing that life-changing message with others. They may need to hear it many times, perhaps even over many years. As kingdom Christians, we keep sharing it with love in our hearts and a prayer on our lips that others can embrace the wonderful truth.

We began this chapter with the story of good ol' Chet, who was such a good man in so many ways, but had not experienced the new birth of his heart. A friend of mine became Chet's pastor about the time Chet's lovely wife of many years went to be with the Lord. It wasn't long before Chet faced a serious health crisis of his own. He was hospitalized with an aneurism near the heart. His young pastor visited him and initiated a conversation about Chet's spiritual needs. He asked if Chet would like to pray. And despite the many prayers Chet had heard across the years, Chet acknowledged that he didn't really know how to pray. His pastor knew that Chet's chances of survival were slim.

There was an urgency about this scene. So the pastor asked Chet if he could pray and let Chet listen to his prayer, and he urged Chet to simply agree in his heart with what he was praying. The pastor prayed a simple yet powerful prayer, acknowledging Chet's desire to become a Christian. He asked Christ to forgive Chet's sin and come into his heart and life. When the prayer was done, there was a calm peace as ol' Chet affirmed that he had heard the prayer and agreed. In his heart that day, Chet became a new man, born again as he finally accepted the grace Christ offered.

Chet never recovered and died several days later in surgery. Before he died, he told his son what had happened when the preacher prayed with him. While it's a shame that Chet never took that step of faith years before so he could have enjoyed the benefits of Christian life on this earth, the angels in heaven surely rejoiced the day Chet became a new man—the day Chet was born again.

Kingdom Christians must first be spiritually alive— born anew. Do you desire to be a kingdom Christian? The Lord offers that work of grace to each of us—and the good news of the gospel is that every one of us can experience it!

Scripture Cited: John 3:3-8, 16; 2 Corinthians 5:17

About the Author: Dr. Pusey is senior pastor of First Church of the Nazarene in Kansas City, Missouri.

TRUTH TO REMEMBER

Kingdom Christians are growing
"in the grace and knowledge
of our Lord and Savior Jesus Christ."

SPIRITUALLY GROWING

BY MARK HOLMES

It had become a common experience while learning to fly. My instructor would reach over and pull the plane's throttle back until the motor idled powerlessly. It would be my responsibility to maneuver the craft for an emergency landing without touching the throttle. The procedure did not require that I actually land the plane, merely convince my instructor that I could. Once he was satisfied with my approach, he would give the OK, and I would push the throttle in, bringing the motor roaring back to life, and with the renewed power, climb back to a safer altitude above the ground. However, on this occasion, when I pushed the throttle in, in place of the customary roar, there was a cough, a sputter, and then silence. Now, I have had a number of sounds capture my attention over my lifetime, but nothing has grabbed my interest like that sound. There are two words that do not go well when flying—low and slow—and we were both of these over an unknown farmer's field. Fortunately, the sound also captured my instructor's attention, causing him to seize control of the craft, and rescue me from making unnecessary "ruts" in the ground. I learned a fundamental truth about flying from this experience—planes do not maintain altitude without power. There is no middle ground. You are either moving ahead under power or you are on your way down.

The same is true for the Christian life. One cannot coast into the Kingdom. If you are not growing, you are dying. There is no complacent middle ground. Kingdom Christians are aware of this and have discovered the joy of keeping their spiritual motors purring, experiencing the exhilaration of the climb to higher levels with God.

SPIRITUAL GROWTH IS HOLISTIC

One of my first encounters with a true kingdom Christian was J. C. McPheeters at Asbury Theological Seminary. Already in his late 80s, this "statesman of holiness" had not only developed a legacy with his life of service, but continued to challenge everyone around him to a higher level with God through his lifestyle. Even at his advanced age, his mind was sharp and his body strong. It was nothing for him to join in a game of racquetball or lift weights with students at the school. But more than his physical health, he was in shape spiritually. Keeping with the spirit and discipline of John Wesley, Dr. McPheeters would rise at 4:00 each morning to spend time in prayer, Scripture study, and physical exercise. The results were obvious. From his example, Dr. McPheeters taught me that spiritual growth is a holistic experience, affecting every aspect of one's existence.

Jesus encouraged this holistic approach to spirituality in Mark 12:29-30. He quoted Deuteronomy 6:4, which called Israel to love God with all of their "heart" (emotions), "soul" (spirit), and "strength" (body). Jesus added a fourth dimension, namely the "mind." In addition, Luke described Jesus' maturation in the same way: He "grew in wisdom [mentally] and stature [physically], and in favor with God [spiritually] and men [socially]" (2:52).

All of these aspects come together to make up what we understand to be our identity. If any of these expressions is left out, our identity becomes distorted. Such is true with our maturity as a Christian. We cannot fixate on one aspect at the cost of another. The common temptation is to consider the spiritual portion of our life while ignoring the physical, mental, emotional, and social parts of our existence, failing to see the significance of these other areas to our spiritual health. The result is seen in a distorted and confusing development where we remain undeveloped in some areas, and muscle-bound in others.

The distortion can develop inner conflict over time, producing a confusing experience in one's walk with God. In keeping with Jesus' teaching and example, any attempt to mature as a Christian must be holistic in scope. Within our practice of the commonly accepted spiritual disciplines of prayer, Bible study, fasting, meditation, etc., we must find ways of stimulating our minds, exercising our bodies, developing and controlling our emotions, as well as relating to the world around us.

WHAT IS GOD'S PART?

Hopefully, what I have written so far has served to inspire you to reactivate your Christian development. However, before you begin your growth process, I have a question to ask: What will make this present attempt any different than those of your past?

We all have experienced times when we have made a conscious effort toward spiritual growth. We start with the best of intentions. We set goals, determine methods, and start out with zeal, only to find our interests wane within a short period of time, leaving us with the uncomfortable realization that we are not doing what we intended. So, we tell ourselves that we will get started again someday when we have more time, energy, or whatever.

How can we prevent this new attempt from ending as before?

The answer to our propensity to lapse back into inactivity is to take advantage of God's provisions. They are always available for the Christian; we can just be unaware of their existence. We enter into our new disciplines with a distorted concept picturing God standing on the sidelines of life, watching us develop our spiritual perspiration and stamina, waiting for the time when we achieve our goal of maturity, so He can come over to us and congratulate us for our accomplishments. But God refuses to be on the sidelines of our life. He desires to be in the midst of our activities, helping us to achieve all that He has for us and more. To aid us, God has provided ways of helping us to do what we could not do on our own. These are introduced to us by the apostle Peter in 2 Peter 3:18, "Grow in the grace and knowledge of our Lord and Savior Jesus Christ." The provisions of God are *grace* and *knowledge*. Without these, we are left to achieve our growth by human ability, the cause of many of our past failures.

GRACE

Christians talk a lot about grace. However, our understanding of the word can be rather limited. To most, grace means unmerited favor. It is the means by which we are relieved by God of our responsibility for sin. However, the application of grace is far more broad and beneficial.

Grace is a figurative space within which the believer dwells. It stands in contrast to where we were before salvation. We were under law, dominated by sin, estranged from God. But having been made a child of God, we moved into the arena of grace, which sets us free from the law, delivers us from sin, and unites us with God. It is an existence where we experience a freedom found nowhere else, a freedom that allows us latitude for our spiritual growth.

Grace is also a means of empowerment, enabling us to do what we could not do by any other means. It carries the sense of one who is stronger coming to the aid of the weak. Where we have not been able to attain our spiritual goals by our own strength, we can, empowered by God's grace.

Where is God in your spiritual growth process? Is He on the sidelines watching your best efforts, patiently waiting for you to achieve maturity; or is He involved with you, providing the arena where you work and the power by which it is achieved? God is a participator, not a spectator. He is involved through enabling us to grow, providing the stamina to continue when otherwise we would quit. Grace is more than God providing an accepting attitude toward us. It is God interacting, empowering, and changing us as we open ourselves to His provisions. Are you open to the full benefits of God's grace for your life?

KNOWLEDGE

Just as we err in our limitation of grace, we can also misunderstand the place of God's knowledge in our spiritual growth. Some assume that spiritual maturity is revealed by the amount of knowledge one has attained. If a person knows the Bible "inside and out," we assume he or she is spiritually mature. Nevertheless, we have all encountered people who may be able to cite chapter and verse, but at the same time exhibit a nature and behavior devoid of any spiritual quality. In short, there is quite a difference between knowing things *about* the Savior and *knowing* the Savior. Knowledge is necessary for growing spiritually, but not all knowledge is beneficial.

A second error is the assumption that knowledge deals with how to behave. The idea is, the better we understand the rules, the more "Christian" we will live. A popular attempt at this was the WWJD campaign that had many of us sporting bracelets and lapel pins to jog our memory to ask at the moment of decision, "What would Jesus do?" Certainly this served as a means by which people could make better decisions and relate more wholesome responses to the challenges of the world. However, growing spiritually is not about learning the rules; it is about being changed into the likeness of God. It is not about action; it's about being. *Acting* like Jesus is not synonymous with *becoming* like Jesus. The distinction is found in the essence of one's nature. Following a list of rules, expectations, and understandings will only result in making us obedient; it will do little about who we really are inwardly. To grow into kingdom Christians, we must be *trans*formed, not just *con*formed. This is why the apostle Paul challenged us to "be transformed by the renewing of [our] minds" (Romans 12:2). What we do should be motivated by our natures from within, not a list of rules from without. Einstein once said, "I want to think the thoughts of God; everything else is commentary." To grow in the knowledge of God takes us a step deeper than action to that of becoming. Acting mimics; knowing transforms.

There is no more direct application of this teaching than Philippians 2:5, where Paul instructs us to have the same mind, or "attitude," that existed in Jesus. Specifically, he speaks of humility and obedience. While having Christ's mind is not limited to these two expressions, they are central to any success in spiritual maturity. Without humility and obedience, the influence and power of God in our lives become contradictory, creating a battleground in place of communion. The important distinction, though, is to realize the source of one's humility and obedience is transformation of the inner person.

As I look back over my life, I can think of a few people who had discovered the joy of growing spiritually into kingdom Christians. Each one exhibited his or her own unique expression of the grace and knowledge of Christ.

I met Leisel when I became the pastor of her church. Leisel was an elderly widow who lived alone in the farm country of western Pennsylvania. She was a lady of simple means, depicting a no-nonsense, almost legalistic air about her. But first impressions were far from accurate. As I came to know this lady of God, I found in her one who not only knew about grace but also exhibited it in her everyday life.

There were certain things that our church participated in that were contradictory to Leisel's convictions. Yet, she lived in harmony with those who did not hold her views, allowing the same latitude among the congregation that God graciously had extended to her. Her modest lifestyle could easily be understood as caused by a widow's pension. I do not know what Leisel's income was, but I know she willingly did without many of the world's trappings so she could provide for the work of God at home and around the world. She had a humility and insight that expressed the presence of God, which I found comforting. I admit, when I would visit with Leisel, it felt like a reversed pastor-parishioner relationship. I was the one who came away enriched and blessed as she exhibited, quite without her knowing, the presence of God to me. Leisel knew Christ and exercised His grace, living as a lady who had the mind and heart of God.

Theodore was a retired minister in another of my churches. A widower in his late 80s, he was a man of energy, grace, and ingenuity. His mind was alive with ideas, causing him to spend his days creating objects of art, developing a small museum-like display of woodcutting tools, and even building an enormous seesaw that would lift a person over 10 feet in the air. (This was dismantled at the insistence of his daughters after a group of children riding it with him suddenly got off their side, bringing him crashing to earth.)

Beyond his love for life, Theodore revealed a godly insight into the world. He manifested a wisdom that gently caused persons to rethink their view of life. An illustration of this was an observation he once made regarding the popular use of personal music devices within society. He believed people were robbing themselves of opportunities to hear the voice of God by allowing their world to be constantly invaded by sounds that prevented the awareness of the Master's voice. As a man who spent considerable time in communion with God, such a lifestyle seemed foreign to him. He felt that people were exhibiting a fear of silence, where God could speak clearly to them. It was not that he was against the devices or music itself. Rather, for him, the music of the soul was not developed through electrical impulses, but in the Voice he had come to know within that sphere of grace in which he walked each day with God.

I am sure we can all think of kingdom Christians who exhibit godly personalities through the maturity they have attained over a life of fellowship with our Savior. It is a level that we can all attain, if we avail ourselves to the provisions of grace and knowledge that come from God. But it must be an intentional effort that involves the entirety of our being. Growth and maturity do not come by complacency. Despite what we may think, we cannot glide into the kingdom of God.

So, how is your spiritual motor running? Is it idling? sputtering? Or is it at full power, climbing to new heights with God, becoming a kingdom Christian?

Scripture Cited: Deuteronomy 6:4; Mark 12:29-30; Luke 2:52; Romans 12:2; Philippians 2:5; 2 Peter 3:18

About the Author: Rev. Holmes is senior pastor of The Wesleyan Church in Superior, Wisconsin.

TRUTH TO REMEMBER

Kingdom Christians practice spiritual discipline.

4

SPIRITUALLY PREPARED

BY ERIC FORGRAVE

Allen Iverson, talented guard for the Philadelphia 76ers basketball team, once told the sports media that people shouldn't be upset about him missing basketball practice or make him feel *guilty* about it. "We're talking practice," he repeated several times. In his mind, practice is *only* practice. What is really important is the game. As a gifted athlete, practice for Iverson seems to be an *unnecessary* evil.

NOT ANOTHER GUILT TRIP

"Guilty" is a good word to describe the way many followers of Jesus feel about "practicing" spiritual discipline. The term "spiritual discipline" brings to mind that most of us feel inadequate in those areas. Most of us know we need to or should pray *more*, read the Bible *more*, spend *more* time telling our kids God's story, *more* time fasting, *more* time practicing spiritual discipline—more, more, more.

However, "more" is a life-draining word. "More" is a word that implies our best efforts are never enough. "More" makes us feel guilty about our relationship with God. "More" eventually turns spiritual discipline into a necessary obligation (just something we do because we are supposed to), like eating all our vegetables before getting dessert. Like mowing the lawn. Like paying bills.

A good indication that devotional times are motivated

by guilt or obligation is the oppressive feeling of being a failure if we miss a day or if our prayer time isn't powerful or spiritually moving. Daily devotional times, though good and valuable and even essential, have unfortunately become *the* litmus test for a good relationship with God for many Christians, and—if we are honest with ourselves—a way of earning favor with God.

Please understand that I am not saying that we should abandon the spiritual disciplines. But I am saying that when the spiritual disciplines are *the* measuring tape of our Christianity, we set ourselves up for resignation, puddle-deep (instead of ocean-deep) transformation, and even for resentment toward God. What's the alternative, then? Move from obligation to what? Trying harder? No. Giving up? No. Restlessness? Yes, restlessness!

Restlessness, not in the sense of tossing and turning at night (although it might include that), but in the sense of *not being able to do anything else with a clear heart and mind until some space has been made for God.* The space may possibly be created through prayer; Bible-reading; a prayer walk; spiritual reading *(lectio divina);* corporate worship; confession; ministering to and serving others by listening, caring, coming alongside; silence; etc.

How is this different from guilt and obligation? Guilt and obligation are negative motivations that usually come from others: a well-meaning Sunday School teacher, a pastor, a parent, or from our own unmet expectations. I remember, when I was a youngster, one pastor saying to the congregation, "Shame on you!" from the pulpit. If that's not a guilt trip, I don't know what is. I don't remember what we were supposed to be ashamed of, but I do remember those words of guilt and shame 20 years later. Many Christians can retell that story in a myriad of ways when it comes to the spiritual disciplines as they continue to deal with the effects of and be motivated by lingering guilt.

Restlessness is brought to our hearts by God. Restlessness

may come as the inability to pray or not knowing what to pray or weightiness of heart. Restlessness is a warning signal that blares, "Pay attention to your heart!" Restlessness is awareness that things are out of whack without God, a hunger and thirst to be in His presence, and recognition that rest is only found in Him. As Augustine prayed, "Thou hast made us for thyself, O Lord; and our heart is restless until it rests in thee."*

Spiritual discipline (paying attention), then, is the practice of nurturing sensitivity to that restlessness (God's voice) in our hearts in order to foster the making of space for God. Paying attention to God's voice creates space for God. That is, God draws us to His embrace through restlessness.

When we are restless, we can pray this prayer: "Help me, Lord, to listen to my heart and life. Help me most of all to listen to You. Unclog my ears and free me of my screening processes and selective hearing that let me hear only the things I want to hear from You. May I know the warmth of Your embrace, and may Your presence deliver me from coldness of heart. Amen."

GOD MANAGEMENT VERSUS FIELDS OF GRACE

Paper I would usually discard I now stuff in a designated recycling paper bag or cardboard box in my office. Sometimes it is weeks before I take the paper out to the yellow recycling Dumpster. Maybe it is because I don't want to deal with the paper right then or don't have time. Still, no matter how full the bag or box gets, I always manage to find room to cram more paper in. It's amazing how heavy accumulated paper weighs!

Unfortunately, the way I find room for more paper is probably one of the most common ways we try to make space for God in our hyperbusy lives. My recycling paper bag is a good picture of most of our lives. I know it is of mine. We look at our lives crammed with responsibilities—places to go, work, appointments, duties around the house, church, school, kids, spouse, friends, meetings, meals—and wonder how we can possibly find *more* room to cram God in. Restlessness tells us that is the wrong question. Isn't that a relief?

Josh, one of the students in our youth ministry, asked me how summer camp went because he was unable to go. I shared with him some of the ways we encountered God during the week. His reply is insightful for our conversation about making space for God. "Yeah, I love camp. It is a time when you can get away from all the distractions in your life and focus on God." That's it! Making space for God in our lives isn't about trying to find *more* room to cram God into our already jam-packed lives. Making space for God is about listening to the restlessness of our hearts and making ourselves, jam-packed lives and all, available to God. Do you see the difference? Trying to find more room to cram God in isn't really about our relationship with God at all; that's God management. We are trying to tell God where He fits in. Any attempt to manage God is an exercise in futility, so it is no surprise that there is so little transformation of our hearts and lives when God is under our supervision.

Just the opposite of trying to find more room to cram God in, paying attention to the warning signals of our restlessness—weightiness of heart, the inability to pray, things being out of whack, a hunger and thirst for God—is the *beginning* of our availability to God. Don't be discouraged if you fall into that first category, if you have been trying to cram God in. That can actually be good news! The restlessness of our hearts perhaps is never more apparent than when we are battling with "more." Pay attention to where God wants to lead through restlessness, because restlessness encourages us not to ask, "How can I find more room to cram God in?" but instead, "Where is the path to God's rest?" By God's grace, we can find ourselves in the pastures of God's mercy and rest, which are available to continually refresh and reaffirm who we are in Christ.

Knowing that, we can pray: "God of all comfort and consolation draw me close to You. Make me lie down in the green pastures of Your grace and rest. Lead me beside still waters that I may hear Your voice. Lead me in paths of righteousness for Your name's sake. May my cup overflow as I am available to You. Amen."

AVAILABLE TO REFRESH

Have you ever worn clothes that didn't fit? Maybe because nothing else is clean. Because they are still your "favorite" pants even though they don't button up anymore. Or because the extra bagginess helps give you a sense of security about your ever-growing waistline. (I am speaking from personal experience.)

David did once, but not for very long.

After being shocked by the blasphemous defiance of Goliath, David was determined to do something about it—to fight and kill Goliath. After hearing about David's courageous grit, Saul sent for him. David suggested that he be the one to stand up to Israel's biggest bully. "Let no one lose heart on account of this Philistine; your servant will go and fight him" (1 Samuel 17:32). On paper, David had no chance. He was "only a boy" (v. 33). However, David's experience protecting his father's sheep from the fiercest of wild animals convinced Saul to let David fight. However, Saul was also convinced that David was going to need some protection in the form of armor. "Then Saul dressed David in his *own* tunic. He put a coat of armor on him and a bronze helmet on his head" (1 Samuel 17:38, emphasis added).

Can you picture it? David was like a five-year-old boy coming out of his parents' closet with his dad's suit and shoes on. He tried walking around in Saul's "protection" but couldn't get used to them. "I cannot go in these" (v. 39). So, David took them off and went to face the Philistine with his shepherd's staff, five smooth stones from a stream, a sling—

and the *Lord's* protection and strength. As David said would happen, the Lord delivered the Philistine into his hand. David's choice: Saul's protection and resources or God's protection and resources. After trying to wear Saul's armor, it was an easy choice. David found strength and the power of deliverance in the Lord.

In conclusion to his letter to the Ephesians, Paul powerfully exhorts the Church to "be strong in the Lord and in his mighty power. Put on the full armor of God" (6:10-11). It is an exhortation to choose God's protection and strength instead of our own or someone else's. The same power that raised Jesus from the dead is available to us to continually refresh our hearts and strengthen our feeble hands. No wonder our hearts are restless when we try to wear "Saul's armor." We are attempting to live out of our own resources instead of being strong in the Lord.

The trouble is, we can do a lot in our own strength and get results. It is easy to get impatient with Kingdom-timing —time for sowing, watering, germinating, growing, and reaping. We think we can get things done much faster and better. I remember a new church that was being built not far from the church I grew up in. It started off well. The foundation was laid, and the cinder block walls were started. It was beginning to look impressive, but then one day construction just stopped. Soon, weeds and grass grew up around the partially constructed walls. Eventually, the land was resold and the partially constructed church building was replaced by a strip mall. I have often wondered what happened. Did they get ahead of God? Did they have their own plans, but God wasn't meeting their timeline, so they went ahead without Him? Did they get impatient and expect God to bless their plans instead of waiting? Who knows for sure, but the half-completed church certainly wasn't a testimony of trust and dependence on God's strength and resources.

Restlessness leads us to the place where wearing anything but God's armor and living out of His resources of strength is like wearing an itchy wool sweater, from a place where we say along with David, "I can't go in these" and to a place of real power. Refreshed and strengthened by grace—that is a good place to be, because it is one of the steps toward reaffirming our identity in Christ.

CUBICLE CHRISTIANITY AND WHOLENESS IN CHRIST

Early in my childhood baseball career, I got the nickname "Triple Man" from one of the coaches. I didn't get this name because I hit dozens of triples or because I could stretch a double into a triple with my lightning quick speed. In fact, early on, I wasn't good at all. I struck out often. One time I even struck out by stepping out of the batter's box to swing at a pitch that would have hit me. But the two hits I do remember getting that season were triples, and one of them came at an important point in the game—a time when coaches wish a kid like me wasn't up to bat. My triple sparked a late-inning rally, and we won the game. After the game, as we slurped our free milkshakes at a fast-food restaurant, my coach dubbed me "Triple Man." "Triple Man" became not only a nickname, but my identity on that team that gave me confidence in the coming years.

In Ephesians, the Church is identified as God's "adopted" children (1:5), "God's possession" (1:14), Christ's "body" (1:23; 4:6, 25; 5:30), "God's workmanship" (2:10), "God's holy people" (5:3), and as "children of light" (5:8). The very fabric of the Church's entire identity is woven with God's initiative and grace. As we graze in God's pastures of rest, we begin to operate out of who we are (adopted children, God's possession, etc.) instead of who we are not or who we used to be. As our identity in Christ is reaffirmed over and over, God's power and strength work out in boldness, steadfastness, and alertness. That is to say, once we are out of "Saul's armor" and as we find our strength in the Lord, the more what we used to be seems foreign and the more what God's calls us to be and do becomes the perfect fit. God in Christ gives us identity. And that identity gives us purpose, acceptance, and worth.

In my work with teenagers, this is a battleground area. It is true of adults as well. Instead of finding and seeing their identity solely and wholly defined in Christ, often teens and people in general think of their identity as a pie—Christ being one piece of the pie along with many other pieces, such as family, work, hobbies, friends, nationality, school, etc. However if Christ is just a piece of the pie, no matter how big that piece is, then our identity is fragmented and compartmentalized like an office building with a hundred different cubicles, each one with its own task and job description. That is not only another picture of God management ("God, here is where You fit in"), but how confusing it is to live that way!

Think of it, instead, in this way. Christ is the crust that holds the pie together. Or Christ is the flavoring that gives the pie its distinctive identity, like cherries make a cherry pie. Our identity in Christ informs and shapes everything else in our lives. We are *Christian* parents; *Christian* teachers, truckers, postal workers, doctors, etc.; *Christians* who enjoy certain hobbies; *Christian* students; and *Christian* Americans (American is not synonymous with Christian)—not the other way around. Our identity is solely wrapped up in Christ. Our relationship with Christ is what informs *all* of our choices and decisions, not just the church-related ones. Our priorities begin to change and the construction of our own kingdoms is not just stalled or to be continued, but stopped, halted, and deconstructed.

Restlessness leads us to the place where compartments are only found in cupboards and drawers, but not in our lives, because our all-encompassing defining identity is in Christ. Restlessness leads us to give up "cubicle Christianity" for wholeness in Christ. Restlessness leads us to clarity about who we are in Christ. And God spreads the unmistakable aroma of Christ through us in every place.

BLESSINGS AND BENEDICTION

As I began to think about how to conclude this chapter, I thought, "What better way than to pass along blessings and benediction?" So, here are some good words to send you forth:

May you be surprised by grace and may you bump into signs of God's goodness to you.
May you find yourself grazing in the pastures of God's rest and mercy.
May God help you to ask the right questions.
May the restlessness of your heart draw you near to the heart of God.
May God make your own resources and armor so uncomfortable that you have to say, "I can't go in these."
May you know that God holds you in His arms and close to His heart.
May you never lose heart, because your confidence and competence is from God.
May God deliver you from the cubicle and grant you wholeness and peace in Christ.
May God free you from the tyranny of shame and guilt brought on you wrongly by others.
May the path to God's rest always be clear to you.
"Finally, be strong in the Lord and in his mighty [resurrection] power" (Ephesians 6:10, see also Ephesians 1:20).
The grace and peace of Christ be yours.

Notes:
*Rueben P. Job and Norman Shawchuck, eds., *A Guide to Prayer* (Nashville: The Upper Room, 1983), 274.

Scripture Cited: 1 Samuel 17:32-33, 38-39; Ephesians 1:5, 23; 2:10; 4:6, 25; 5:3, 8, 30; 6:10

About the Author: Rev. Forgrave is associate pastor of the Grandview (Missouri) Church of the Nazarene.

TRUTH TO REMEMBER

Kingdom Christians think about "excellent" and "praiseworthy" things.

5

PROPER THOUGHT LIVES

BY DARLENE TEAGUE

Where did that come from? The Christian shook her head as she realized she was singing words from a popular song, words that celebrated things that were contrary to her faith and life. *I had no idea that I knew that song.*

With that thought, the Holy Spirit seemed to say, "You pick up the words to songs easily, so you must be careful. That goes for things you choose to listen to and things you find yourself hearing as you go through the day."

She found that it was easier to *know* she needed to guard her ears than actually to *do* it.

* * *

He figured that watching the game was OK for him as a Christian. In fact, his church was having a party during it as a way to connect to some of the people in their neighborhood. He and his family decided to stay home. However as he was watching that night, he realized he was being bombarded with images that triggered lustful thoughts. *Where did that come from?*

He felt the Holy Spirit telling him that he had to be careful about what he let into his mind through his eyes.

* * *

He's always the one who gets the work done first—and best. Just once, I wish he'd mess up royally.

Every time I see her, she looks as if she's just come from a photo shoot for a fashion magazine. Maybe she'll spill spaghetti sauce on that crisp, white blouse. Then we'll see who's picture perfect!

Where did those thoughts come from?

Why is it important for us, as Christians, to guard our thoughts? In fact, do we need to be careful of the things we hold in our heads? After all, what really matters is how we live, right?

CHOOSING WHERE TO FOCUS OUR THOUGHTS

What we hold on to in our minds influences who we become. Paul urges us to be intentional in the things that influence us. Look at what he says in Colossians 3:1–2: "Since you have been raised to new life with Christ, set your sights on the realities of heaven, where Christ sits at God's right hand in the place of honor and power. *Let heaven fill your thoughts.* Do not think only about things down here on earth" (NLT, emphasis added). And in Philippians 4:8: "Fix your thoughts on what is true and honorable and right. Think about things that are pure and lovely and admirable. Think about things that are excellent and worthy of praise" (NLT).

God has transformed us from sinners into His children. He has transformed us from death to life. He has made us new creations in Christ Jesus. Because He has given us life, both now and eternally, we need to refocus our eyes and ears and hearts to the things that are of God. While we have an initial moment when we decide to accept Christ as Savior and Lord, we have to keep on choosing to live for God. We have heaven as a goal, but we have everyday life to live until we get there. You see, we're living in a sinful, fallen world that's under Satan's control. He's battling for our souls, even after we become Christians!

It's a bit like players in a paintball or laser-tag game. One player is on the offensive, trying to tag others. But others are shooting at him or her from all directions. He or she has to be aware of the various dangers around at all times.

So do we; the world's influences are everywhere. From television to music to billboards to magazines to the Internet, we are bombarded with Satan's lies. That's why we have to be spiritually prepared. We're in a daily battle over what goes on in our minds.

Here's a question that would be worth a few moment's reflection: "Would you be embarrassed if your friends and associates knew what went on inside your mind?"

Many would tell us that what we do in private, including our thoughts, is our own business and no one else's. As Christians, we think differently. We make ourselves accountable for how we live *and* how we think. If we're living as kingdom Christians and choosing to focus on thoughts that honor God, we won't be embarrassed by what we're thinking. The psalmist said, "Search me, O God, and know my heart; test me and know my anxious thoughts. See if there is any offensive way in me, and lead me in the way everlasting" (Psalm 139:23–24). God will help us keep our minds focused on the right things. You see, there's danger in letting Satan have victory in any part of our minds.

Two theological students were walking along a street in the Whitechapel district of London, a section where old and used clothing is sold. "What a fitting illustration all this makes!" said one of the students as he pointed to a suit of clothes hanging on a rack by a window. A sign on it read: SLIGHTLY SOILED—GREATLY REDUCED IN PRICE.

"That's it exactly," he continued. "We get soiled by gazing at a vulgar picture, reading a coarse book, or allowing ourselves a little indulgence in dishonest or lustful thoughts. And when the time comes for our character to be appraised, we are greatly reduced in value. Our purity, our strength is gone. We are just part and parcel of the general, shopworn stock of the world."[1]

Yes, continual slight deviations from the path of right may greatly reduce our usefulness to God and to others. In fact, these little secret sins can weaken our character so that when we face a moral crisis, we cannot stand the test. As a result, we go down in spiritual defeat because we have been careless about little sins.

The devil's arrows are going to come. We will be tempted to think unloving, even sinful, thoughts. We don't have to hold on to the ideas that don't please the Lord. Martin Luther said, "We cannot help it if birds fly over our heads. It is another thing if we invite them to build nests in our hats." So it is with the evil that comes to our minds. Let the bad thoughts go; don't keep them or say them.

We need to remember this fact as well: what causes one person to be tempted to evil or wrong thoughts may not be the same thing that tempts someone else. We focus on keeping our own minds pure. Susannah Wesley said, "Whatsoever thing weakens your conscience, that thing for you is sin." For example, in the opening examples, the one person found she had to guard against music that entered her mind so easily. Another person may not have that problem. The man became tempted to lustful thoughts from TV ads. Someone else may see the same ads but not be tempted. The key thing is to be sensitive to the Holy Spirit's voice at all times.

HAVING A PROPER THOUGHT LIFE

Paul gave a good formula for us in winning the battle of our thought lives in Philippians 4:8: "Fix your thoughts on what is true and honorable and right. Think about things that are pure and lovely and admirable. Think about things that are excellent and worthy of praise" (NLT). Let's look more closely at his formula.

Fix your thoughts on what is true. If we're going to fix our thoughts on something, we make a deliberate decision to bring that thing into our minds. You've probably heard before how bankers and agents are able to recognize counterfeit money. It's not because they study the vast array of counterfeits, but because they know what the real stuff is. They know if it's not true legal tender because they're so well-acquainted with the genuine items.

God's Word is true. We choose to fix our thoughts on His Word. By memorizing Scripture verses or passages, reading chapters, or listening to the Bible on tape, we can fill our mind with Truth.

You know, Jesus gave us a great example in how to fight away wrong thoughts when the devil tempted Him in the wilderness. Matthew 4:1–11 gives the account. Each time the devil tempted Jesus to do something that was contrary to God's will and plan, Jesus responded with a verse of Scripture. The devil tried to make Jesus doubt who He was and what God had sent Him to do, but Jesus countered the devil's lies with the truth from the Word of God.

So think on what is true.

Think on what is honorable. It's honorable to want the best for other people. It's honorable to celebrate the good things others say and do. It's honorable to build up and encourage our friends, family, and associates whenever we can. It's honorable to esteem others. It's honorable to focus praise on God and what He does.

Fix your mind on what is right. We need to refute the lies we hear. When a false idea comes to mind, we must intentionally counter it with the right idea. For example, we may have the thought go through our minds that God can't really love us; we're unlovable. That's a lie. The truth is that God loved us—each of us—so much that He sent His Son Jesus to die for us and bring us back into a relationship with Him. So, we must make sure to fix our minds on the right ideas and dismiss the wrong ones.

Focus on things that are pure and lovely and admirable.

When tempted to entertain an ugly thought, turn it around. Keith Drury made a great suggestion in his book, *Disciplines for Ordinary People*. In his chapter "Thought Life," he focused on sexual temptation, but I think several of his ideas are important for any wrong thought.

Dr. Drury suggests that when we're tempted, we should turn that temptation into spiritual energy. He said,

> Do a turnabout on the devil. When he introduces some delectable temptation to you, immediately go to prayer. Not for yourself, but for others. Take your temptation as a signal that Satan would love to have you fall so that he can more easily get at those in your circle of influence. What about your son? Daughter? People in your church? Someone you discipled? Spouse? Congregation? Could they be tempted likewise? Most likely they are. Thus, go to prayer for them, that they will be strong in their similar temptation. This is a great trick to play on Satan. His temptation merely sends you to earnest prayer for others. The more he tempts you, the more you pray—what a clever ploy! What a mighty ministry of intercessory prayer![2]

I like that idea; take what is ugly and turn it into something powerful and pure and lovely—and admirable.

Fill the mind with things that are excellent and worthy of praise. Christian music, inspirational books and articles, tapes of sermons, or other media that focus our minds on the things of God help us keep our minds tuned toward heaven. Does that mean we ought never watch the news or any TV or listen to other kinds of music? Maybe. Maybe not. We better obey if that's what the Spirit of God directs us to do. The question is, are we willing to give up those entertainments that God says to give up? If not, why not?

Some of us may need to make some shifts in our choices so that we can have minds that are fixed, focused, and filled with the things that honor God. Others of us may need to make some drastic changes to protect ourselves from the devil's traps. No matter how long we walk with the Lord, as long as we're on this side of heaven, we'll have to keep on guarding our minds. And as long as we're on this side of heaven, there will be times we need to make shifts in our thinking and times we'll need to make drastic changes in our lives in order to keep in step with the Spirit of God.

You see, we find the things we're looking for, whether a pure mind or a pattern of pleasing ourselves. Here's a little test: Take a look around where you are sitting and find five things that have red in them. Go ahead and do it. With a "red" mind-set, you'll find that red jumps out at you: a red book, red stripes on a flag, red in the carpeting, red flowers, red in your clothing, and so on. In like fashion, we must look for ways to encourage proper thoughts, holy thoughts, heavenly thoughts. We'll find them if we look for them.

Let's consider a few more questions:

How often are we shocked by the images around us? Are we sensitive to things that might cause someone else to stumble in his or her faith?

What do we think about when we're relaxing or not involved in some activity?

What are we reading? Do we have books or magazines or files that we shouldn't have as Christians?

What are we watching on TV (either shows or movies)? Are we careless in viewing violence and loose sexual behavior? Are we exposing our children to things that are contrary to our Christian beliefs and standards?

How often and how much of the Bible did we read last week?

How many times did we consciously put good, godly thoughts into our minds?

How many times did we offer a kind word instead of a critical one?

How many times did we choose to say nothing rather than be hurtful?

Remember our friend at the beginning of the chapter?

She made some shifts in her practices and behavior. She intentionally selected music that helped her keep her thoughts focused on heaven. She discovered that as she listened to Christian or classical music throughout the day, her thoughts frequently turned in praise to the Lord.

Remember our sports fan? He made a radical change in his life. He found himself addicted to TV and the titillating ads. As he sought to focus his mind on the things that pleased God, he had to remove the TV from his home. He knows that at some time, he may be able to bring it in and view wholesome videos or DVDs. For now, he believes that the Lord wants him to set the time he used to watch TV to do extra Bible reading and pray. He wants to set a good example for his children in his choices.

What about you? What can you do this week to make your thought life one that honors God? Will you do it?

May God help us all to live as kingdom Christians and let heaven fill our thoughts!

Notes:

1. <http://www.higherpraise.com/illustrations/purity.htm>

2. Keith Drury, *Spiritual Disciplines for Ordinary People* (Wesleyan Publishing House, 2004), 76.

Scripture Cited: Psalm 119:23-24; Philippians 4:8; Colossians 3:1-2

About the Author: Rev. Teague is an ordained elder in The Wesleyan Church, and a senior editor at the Wesleyan headquarters in Indianapolis.

TRUTH TO REMEMBER

Kingdom Christians solve problems
    with the help of prayer, the Bible,
  and other Christians.

SOLVE PROBLEMS GOD'S WAY

BY MARK LITTLETON

The sermon that Sunday filled Brent with a sense of hope and also fear. How was he to become a "kingdom Christian" in the arena of all his problems? An alcoholic, he had defeated the urge to drink more than 100 times, and then succumbed to it another 200. Yet, the program he entered in church helped. He built some friendships and felt stronger in dealing with the problem of drink. But what about his wife? She wanted a divorce. What about his kids? They acted angry and confused. What about his job situation? All these things were to be dealt with in a "kingdom" way—considering what God wanted and what would build up His kingdom.

On another front, Jackie struggled with some similar issues. However, the big problem before her now was her father. The old man had become incontinent, forgetful, and now he couldn't even walk. A fall had put him into the hospital. Her husband said it was time for the nursing home, but she resisted. Was she doing the right thing, the "kingdom" thing? That morning her pastor had emphasized the idea of being "kingdom Christians." Still, she didn't know of any scriptures she could turn to about nursing homes.

Greg also listened with interest to the message. He didn't have a particular problem at the moment, but he liked the idea of becoming a "kingdom Christian." He wanted to know more. What should he do as an average citizen and church member, a single guy looking for a wife? How could he live out the principles the pastor had outlined?

GOD'S WILL FOR US

Becoming a kingdom Christian involves an arduous, daily process. We must learn to think in terms of loving God with all our heart, soul, mind, and strength. To solve problems, we have to discover ways that come right out of the Bible. And we must seek God in every circumstance.

How do we pull this off?

Knowing God's will on any subject is not always easy. Yet, knowing the Bible well and where to look for answers helps immeasurably. God has given us a number of resources that we can turn to while embroiled in a difficult situation. Here are four tried-and-true methods for discerning God's will on any issue:

1. *What does the Bible say about it?* Second Timothy 3:16-17 tells us, "All scripture is inspired by God and is useful for teaching, for reproof, for correction, and for training in righteousness, so that everyone who belongs to God may be proficient, equipped for every good work" (NRSV). In this passage, we see four things scripture is able to do: (1) teach us—show us what to do in any circumstance; (2) reprove us—point out where we're wrong; (3) correct us—lead us to the right way to handle the problem; and (4) train us in righteousness—give us general training that follows through our entire lives.

Such powerful guidance is available to every Christian. Simply by searching the Scriptures and determining what principles they offer for our direction, we can discover God's way in any situation. For instance, in the scenario above with Brent and his troubles with his family, alcoholism, and so on, he began reading the Bible with an eye to ferreting out what would help him. In one instance, he came to Ephesians 5:18, which told him not to "get drunk on wine, . . . Instead, be

filled with the Spirit." He began seeking the Spirit's control
and power every time he felt the rush of thirst for drink. He
talked to his wife about how God hates divorce (see Malachi
2:16); and as she saw him transform through the impact of
what he learned, she fell in love with him all over again. Passages on discipline of children and raising them up in the
Lord's way helped Brent develop consistency and compassion in his fathering skills. In time, his three children all rec-
ognized that their father was a new man, and they also
wanted to live as kingdom Christians.

God's Word has power "sharper than any double-edged
sword," according to Hebrews 4:12; and it can cut right
through all the garbage the world piles up on us to keep us
from seeing the truth. As Psalm 1 says,

> Blessed is the man who does not walk in the coun-
> sel of the wicked or stand in the way of sinners or sit in
> the seat of mockers. But his delight is in the law of the
> LORD, and on his law he meditates day and night. He is
> like a tree planted by streams of water, which yields its
> fruit in season and whose leaf does not wither. Whatev-
> er he does prospers (vv. 1-3).

Not only did Brent find that refusing to live by the "counsel
of the wicked" or the "way of sinners" was more healthy for
him, he also discovered true "delight" in meditating on God's
Word. As a result, his family began to "prosper" in ways he'd
never expected or hoped.

This leads to a second principle of discerning God's
will:

2. *Have we prayed about it?* Many scriptures combine to
give us clear insight into the power of prayer in learning
God's directives. For instance, James 5:16 warns us to "confess your sins to one another, and pray for one another, so
that you may be healed. The prayer of the righteous is powerful and effective" (NRSV).

What is this verse teaching? For one thing, the necessity
of confession of sin to gain spiritual, emotional, and physical

healing. Admitting to and agreeing with God that sin is sin, that we must turn away from it and repent of it, is an essential. We can't effectively pursue the will of God when we allow sin to dominate our lives.

Looking at what Greg was experiencing above, a good indicator for him as a single person was whom he was dating. At first as a Christian, he never gave a thought to whether the ladies he went out with believed similarly to him. Yet gradually, after several dates in which the women in question were quite put off that Greg would not go to bed with them, he realized he needed to reexamine his priorities. He began studying the Bible and praying about it. When he came to the issue of James 5:16, he confessed to the Lord that his attitude was wrong. He needed to begin dating only Christian women. As a result, he got involved with the singles group at church. There, he met several excellent ladies and began dating them, leaving behind the problems of sex and fornication because they believed, like him, that intercourse should be reserved only for marriage.

We should remember not only to pray by ourselves, though, but as James says, "to confess your sins to one another." That means other Christians listening in and supporting us with prayer as well.

This brings us to a third principle:

3. *What do other Christians say about the problem?* Second Corinthians 1:4 praises God, "who comforts us in all our troubles, so that we can comfort those in any trouble with the comfort we ourselves have received from God." What is the point of this passage?

Paul means that when we are troubled, we receive comfort from God for a distinct purpose: so that we might offer comfort to others in the same way when they go through dire circumstances.

Consider what Solomon says in Proverbs 15:22: "Plans fail for lack of counsel, but with many advisers they succeed." When we consult with different people of faith, often good advice comes to the surface. We find that God leads us to the best action through examining several different options from different advisers. This is how most problem-solving groups operate. Going it alone is not helpful.

When Jackie faced the hospitalization of her father, she prayed about it fervently, studied her Bible, listened to her husband, and tried desperately to come to terms with what she felt she needed to do. Still, it wasn't until she met with her support group at church that a breakthrough occurred. There, several friends of hers, people she'd prayed with for years, offered strong advice. One told her about his experience with his mother in a nursing home. "You have to visit often and at different times," he said, "to make sure they're really taking care of her. Even the best ones won't give her the kind of care you would."

Another said, "Look around at several in your area. All will have different prices and a different way of doing things. To find the best one for your dad calls for some real leg work. You should visit at least five before you make a decision."

Someone else told her about the financial situation. "Medicare doesn't pay for long-term care, but Medicaid will. However, you have to liquidate all your dad's finances and sell his home before Medicaid will help. Unfortunately, whatever estate he has will be eaten up with expenses."

And then a fourth said, "We tried to take care of my mom at home, but it was very wearing. With both my husband and me working, we just couldn't take care of her, even with using some outside services. It's a hard decision, but you have to remember that many nursing homes, when it comes to expertise and ability to do certain things, provide far better care than you would. Maybe you could give your dad a late meal, or sit with him in front of the fireplace. But he'll wear you down. It's 24/7, and it's very tough on most families."

Jackie finally made her decision. They tried having her father in her home, but he simply was beyond their ability. He needed constant changing of diapers, he hollered at night about people from his past coming to help him, and he maintained a grumpy, thankless attitude. In time, Jackie simply had to admit her friends' advice was right. She'd have to put him in full-time care.

Finding out God's will is not easy. Sometimes we misfire. Sometimes we haven't really listened. Sometimes we don't even want to do what He counsels. But becoming a true kingdom Christian means seeking His guidance on everything, even the little things. When we follow the scriptural guidelines above, we'll find that it gets easier and easier to discern what He desires. Pleasing Him will become a daily habit, and life will become good, fulfilling, and effective.

Scripture Cited: Psalm 1:1-3; Proverbs 15:22; 2 Corinthians 1:4; Ephesians 5:18; 2 Timothy 3:16-17; Hebrews 4:12; James 5:16

About the Author: Rev. Littleton is a freelance writer living in Gladstone, Missouri, with his wife, Jeannette, and their children.

TRUTH TO REMEMBER

Kingdom Christians are mentally balanced,
psychologically healthy.

7

PSYCHOLOGICALLY HEALTHY

BY RANDY T. HODGES

Chippie—that's Chippie the parakeet—never saw it coming. One second he was peacefully perched in his cage, sending a song into the air; the next second he was sucked in, washed up, and blown over.

His problem began when his owner decided to clean his cage with a vacuum. She stuck the nozzle in to suck up the seeds and feathers in the bottom of the cage. Suddenly, the nearby telephone rang. Instinctively, she turned to pick it up. She barely said hello when—ssswwwwwppppp! Chippie got sucked in. She gasped, let the phone drop, and snapped off the vacuum. With her heart in her mouth, she unzipped the bag.

There was Chippie—alive, but stunned—covered with heavy black dust. She grabbed him and rushed to the bathtub, turned on the faucet full blast, and held Chippie under a torrent of ice-cold water, power-washing him clean. Then it dawned on her that Chippie was soaking wet and shivering. So, she did what any compassionate pet owner would do: she snatched up the hair dryer and blasted him with hot air.

Did Chippie survive? Yes, but he doesn't sing much anymore. He just sits and stares a lot. It's not hard to see why. Sucked in, washed up, and blown over! It's enough to steal the song from any stout heart.[1]

Ever feel sucked in, washed up, and blown over? For many, it is easy to relate to Chippie. We understand why his song has departed and he just sits and stares. In the midst of the impact of life, we somehow need to find a way to maintain and renew our balance. How can we regain our mental balance and equilibrium in an unsettling world?

A GOOD STARTING POINT

Getting a handle on the target issues in keeping our psychological health is a challenge in itself. Even experts in the field of psychology differ in defining mental health. Oddly, one oft-seen definition is this: "Mental health is the absence of mental illness." That's not extremely helpful, is it?

However, after sifting through many writings on mental health, several criteria emerge that differentiate healthy minds from unhealthy ones. Let's use these seven conditions to form a working definition of mental health:

1. Mentally healthy persons think rationally.

Rational thought, by definition, is thought that makes sense. Being logical and coherent, it builds on a basic understanding of reality in the world. Individuals who are mentally healthy work with reality in understanding and shaping responses to their world.

2. Mentally healthy persons relate effectively.

Someone remarked that self-absorbed people talk to you about themselves. Gossips talk to you about others, and brilliant conversationalists talk to you about you. Those that learn to relate effectively certainly have a leg up in life.

The ability to interact with those around us in a manner that promotes healthy relationships is a trait of sound mental health. This ability to relate effectively includes respecting others, even as we respect ourselves. It involves loving, caring, and considering what others may be feeling.

3. Mentally healthy persons feel appropriately.

Emotion is an essential part of being genuinely human that adds joy and zest to all areas of our life. But emotions can be hard to control. Sometimes, we feel happy and alert. At other times, we feel sad and drained. When saying that mentally healthy persons feel appropriately, we mean that typically our emotional response fits with the circumstances we face. For example, if we've just received a well-deserved compliment, we should feel a sense of satisfaction. Or, if the family pet has just died, it is appropriate to feel sadness at the loss.

4. *Mentally healthy persons function acceptably.*

To function acceptably is to possess the ability to consider the situation and circumstances around us and to respond in a manner that is consistent with what is happening around us. If after a long day's work, we plop down in front of the TV to catch a few minutes of Monday Night Football, we function acceptably. But if our neighbor screams, "The house is on fire!" and we remain glued to the television, we are not functioning acceptably—even if our team is about to score the winning touchdown!

5. *Mentally healthy persons cope satisfactorily, possessing both resilience and flexibility.*

The problems of life require resilience. It might be illustrated by comparing two rubber bands. The first is new and stretchy. When stretched and then released, it quickly returns to its previous shape and size. The second rubber band is older. It has lost its ability to bounce back. Stretch this rubber band, and instead of a supple flexibility, it snaps. Why? It has lost its resilience.

Handling life's challenges demands both flexibility and the ability to bounce back. Without these abilities, we cannot cope for long. Mentally healthy persons possess flexibility and resilience.

6. *Mentally healthy persons control themselves responsibly.*

A friend of mine returned from his physician with the news that he was diabetic. The doctor had explained that from this point on, his lifestyle would have to follow certain regimens. Not only would he have to monitor his blood glucose level, but he would have to discipline himself, restricting what foods he would eat. The doctor explained that if he failed to exercise self-control, there could be severe long-term consequences, including blindness or amputation.

As in my friend's case, sometimes our physical health demands certain types of self-control. But in reality, all of life requires that we control ourselves responsibly or face the consequences. Mentally healthy persons know how to control themselves responsibly.

7. *Mentally healthy persons choose wisely.*

Of course, life is filled with choices, but choosing wisely is essential. It involves considering both the short- and long-range impact of our decisions.

Oswald Chambers says it this way, "Our destiny is not determined *for* us, but it is determined *by* us. Man's free will is part of God's sovereign will. We have freedom to take which course we choose, but not freedom to determine the end of that choice. God makes clear what He desires. We must choose, and the result of the choice is not the inevitableness of law, but the inevitableness of God."[2]

What might we as kingdom Christians do to develop a stronger, more secure base of psychological health? How can we develop our mental balance so we can live in the most God-honoring way possible? It is fascinating that God chose to reveal His instruction manual for living to us using not the language of psychology, but rather the language of love. In Christ Jesus, God reveals to us a fully balanced and healthy life.

JUST WHO IS JESUS?

Jesus models for us both mental balance and psychological health. Let's pause to reflect on who Jesus is. The Early Church struggled to understand how best to speak of Christ. Some over-emphasized His humanity at the expense of His divinity. Others focused on His Godness, while minimizing His humanity. What was right? What was wrong? How do we correctly understand Jesus?

The New Testament presents Jesus as both Son of God (divine) and Son of Man (human). However, it does not try to reconcile these facts. Consider these verses that emphasize Christ's Godness:

- John 1:1, "In the beginning was the Word, and the Word was with God, and the Word was God."
- Colossians 1:15, "He is the image of the invisible God, the firstborn over all creation."
- Colossians 1:19, "For God was pleased to have all his fullness dwell in him."

Jesus existed "in the beginning." "He is the image of the invisible God," and God revealed all His fullness in Jesus Christ. Scripture insists Jesus is divine. However, look also at these verses which focus on Christ's humanity:

- John 1:14, "The Word became flesh and made his dwelling among us. We have seen his glory, the glory of the One and Only, who came from the Father, full of grace and truth."
- Galatians 4:4-5, "But when the time had fully come, God sent his Son, born of a woman, born under law, to redeem those under law, that we might receive the full rights of sons."
- Philippians 2:5-8, "Your attitude should be the same as that of Christ Jesus: Who, being in very nature God, did not consider equality with God something to be grasped, but made himself nothing, taking the very nature of a servant, being made in human likeness. And being found in appearance as a man, he humbled himself and became obedient to death—even death on a cross!"

Jesus "became flesh," "was born of a woman," "was made in human likeness," and was "found in appearance as a man." While the New Testament insists that Jesus is divine, it also presents Him as completely human—just like you and me.

Over time, the struggle of comprehending and correctly explaining Jesus grew until the Church was forced to clearly state who Jesus is. The Church's conclusion is that Jesus is both fully God and fully human. This now-historic understanding actually proves quite helpful. When we look at Jesus, we see in one person at one time both the fullness of

God and the fullness of humanity. H. Ray Dunning comments, "In Jesus Christ, we perceive the full measure of manhood, undeformed by sin."[3] With this understanding, we can affirm that Jesus, the perfect God-Man, models for us both mental balance and psychological health.

JESUS IS OUR MODEL

Using our working definition of mental health, let's consider some examples of how Jesus models for us mental health and psychological balance:

1. *Jesus models what it is to think rationally.*

An incident in the life of Jesus gives us a fascinating glimpse into our Lord's thought process. In Matthew 21:23-27, we find Him well into His ministry. Our Lord was experiencing growing hostility from the Jewish religious establishment. Fearing that Jesus would undermine their authority, leaders came questioning Jesus, not to get information, but rather to trap Him into saying something they could use against Him.

On the surface, their question seemed innocent enough. "By what authority are you doing these things?" they asked (Matthew 21:23). But spotting their trap, Jesus realized that if He claimed that His authority came from God, He would be condemned for blasphemy. It was a heinous sin, which under Jewish law was punishable by death. On the other hand, if Jesus confessed that He was merely acting on His own authority, He would be discredited. Perhaps Jesus' mind flashed back to the warning He gave His disciples: "I am sending you out like sheep among wolves. Therefore be as shrewd as snakes and as innocent as doves" (Matthew 10:16). Snarling wolves were clawing at His door!

Realizing their evil intent and deftly side-stepping their trap, Jesus responded with His own question—one that left His attackers in the same no-win position they had hoped would trap Him. And since they refused to answer His question, Jesus chose to not answer theirs. Thinking clearly and rationally enabled Jesus to avoid the trap laid for Him before God's time for His great sacrifice had arrived.

"That's fine for Jesus," we might acknowledge, "but I'm just not that quick. Give me enough time and I may think of a good response, but I don't always think as fast as I would like." Who doesn't feel like this? Still, the promise Jesus made to His disciples as He prepared them (and us) for the challenges ahead should encourage us: "But when they arrest you, do not worry about what to say or how to say it. At that time you will be given what to say, for it will not be you speaking, but the Spirit of your Father speaking through you" (Matthew 10:19-20).

When we obediently and faithfully rely on God to guide us, He will enable us to both think and respond more rationally than we could imagine. We can trust Him!

2. Jesus shows us what it is to feel appropriately.

In John 11, we read of Jesus raising Lazarus from the dead. It's an unusual story. Unusual not just for the miraculous outcome, but unusual for the emotions that Jesus displays. Jesus twice tells His disciples that He will soon bring Lazarus back to life.

When He heard that his friend Lazarus was ill, Jesus said, "This sickness will not end in death. No, it is for God's glory so that God's Son may be glorified through it" (John 11:4).

But that word was not enough. As the Holy Spirit directs John to record this incident, it is as if He wants to make absolutely clear that the disciples then (and we today) have no room for misunderstanding that Jesus is about to do something totally awesome. He is about to make a dead man live.

After he had said this, he went on to tell them, "Our friend Lazarus has fallen asleep; but I am going there to wake him up." His disciples replied, "Lord, if he sleeps, he will get better." Jesus had been speaking of his death, but his disciples thought he meant natural sleep. So then he told them plainly, "Lazarus is dead" (John 11:11-14). Jesus is quite sure of the situation. He knows that Lazarus is not sleeping, not comatose—but dead. And Jesus also knows that his dead friend is not going to stay dead, but rather is going to be brought back to life. Knowing what Jesus knew, it would have been comprehendible if Jesus had stayed emotionally detached. Jesus could understandably have not gotten too concerned about the death of Lazarus. After all, he was about to be brought back to life.

Nevertheless, the incident grows even more fascinating. Even though Jesus clearly knows that His dead friend Lazarus will momentarily be alive again, Jesus is overcome by the emotion of it all.

When Mary reached the place where Jesus was and saw him, she fell at his feet and said, "Lord, if you had been here, my brother would not have died." When Jesus saw her weeping, and the Jews who had come along with her also weeping, he was deeply moved in spirit and troubled. "Where have you laid him?" he asked. "Come and see, Lord," they replied. Jesus wept (John 11:32-35).

Something about death hurts. Even when long-term believers who have faithfully lived their days in the service of their Savior and Lord die, death hurts. Yes, there is something of a celebration when a saint goes home. There is joy in knowing that the departed believer is now at home, in a better place, no longer hurting or suffering, and with the Lord. There is the triumph of the journey completed.

But there is also pain. There is the grief of loneliness. There is the realization that life is not (and never will be) the same. Even in the best of situations, death hurts. Jesus knows this. Jesus felt this. This is why Jesus was "deeply moved in spirit and troubled." This is why "Jesus wept."

This passage undoubtedly demonstrates that Jesus is God. He demonstrates power over death. Yet, in exposing to us the emotions of Jesus, God reveals that grief and sorrow are natural and normal responses to the pain of loss. God is telling us that for the mentally balanced and psychologically healthy person, it is totally acceptable to give full vent to our pain and hurt when death knocks on our door. If our Lord Jesus Christ hurt with those who hurt, even when He was about to raise the dead back to life, it is fully understandable that when we lose someone we care about deeply, we show it. It's a part of what it means to feel appropriately, to be psychologically healthy, to be human.

GOD CALLS US TO BE LIKE JESUS

I sometimes wonder. I wonder if, like Jesus, we learned to rely more on God and less on ourselves, we would be stronger and more psychologically balanced. I wonder if, like Jesus, we obeyed God completely all the time, we would experience new and deeper levels of mental health. I wonder if, like Jesus, we learned to lovingly give of ourselves sacrificially, we would lose some of the emotional hang-ups that seem to plague us in modern life. I wonder.

I strongly suspect that there are depths of Christlikeness that we have never before considered. And with these come deeper blessings from God that we have not yet imagined. Still, of this we can be certain: In the work of Christ Jesus, we have been freed from the power of sin. We have been freed to offer ourselves to God. We have been freed to love both God and others. And we have been freed to become the people God created us to be. God wants us, as His beloved people, to be mentally balanced and psychologically healthy.

Notes:

1. Gary Carr, *Preacher's Magazine* (January-February 1996), 43.

2. *Draper's Quotations for the Christian World,* (Carol Stream, IL: Tyndale House Publishers, 1992), 1149.

3. H. Ray Dunning, *Grace, Faith and Holiness* (Kansas City: Beacon Hill Press of Kansas City, 1988), 305.

Scripture Cited: Matthew 10:16, 19-20; John 1:1, 14; 11:4, 11-14, 32-35; Galatians 4:4-5; Philippians 2:5-8; Colossians 1:15, 19

About the Author: Dr. Hodges is senior pastor of Hernando (Florida) Church of the Nazarene.

TRUTH TO REMEMBER

Kingdom Christians are the same persons
privately as they are publicly.

THE SAME—INSIDE AND OUT

BY CARL M. LETH

She was, to all appearances, a model of Christian charity. For years, she had regularly gone to the home of a disabled man. She had done all those unpleasant cleaning tasks that needed to be done for someone who could not do them for himself. For the sake of charity, she had gone places most of us wouldn't want to go. She hadn't gone for money. It wasn't a job. It was her faith in action. It was often distasteful and never enjoyable, but always an offering of service.

Then one day in a study group, she discovered in a new way the idea of grace: God's unmerited favor which cannot be earned but only received as a gift—regardless of the virtue of our actions. They were exploring the mystery of salvation by grace rather than works. For some reason in that setting, a new light came on, and she "got it." Well, sort of. She echoed back the idea that God gives us grace that we cannot earn to be sure she understood it. Assured that she had understood it correctly, her surprising response was an expression of frustration and anger. "Do you mean," she exclaimed, "that I have been cleaning that nasty old man's house all these years for nothing!"

Like many of us, she was unclear about the relationship of God's gift of grace and the call to a lifestyle of godly discipleship. So, what does it mean to be a kingdom Christian? How do we connect the discovery of grace and the life of faith?

KINGDOM CITIZENSHIP

God's call to us is neither an offer of cheap grace nor a charge to earn our salvation by works of charity. It is a call to become a citizen of His kingdom. Our challenge is to understand—and then express—what that means. Citizenship in the Kingdom means more than having a name on a passport or an address in a particular geographic location. It means sharing in the character of God's life. "But just as he who called you is holy, so be holy in all you do; for it is written: 'Be holy, because I am holy'" (1 Peter 1:15-16).

When Peter named this idea as the centerpiece of kingdom citizenship, he wasn't creating a new concept or proposing a novel idea. He was echoing God's repeated call through the history of the people of Israel. We, like the people of Israel, are often guilty of misunderstanding the central issue in God's special history with His people as the land of Israel. Although much of the Old Testament story revolves around the land that He provided them, the heart of the story is not about God's call to a *land* but to a *life*. In Leviticus 11:45, God connects these two parts of the story. "I am the LORD who brought you up out of Egypt to be your God; therefore be holy, because I am holy." The point was never about a place, but about being a particular people.

To be a kingdom Christian is to be a person who reflects the character of God's life—His holy life. That is more than something we do or something we say. It is who and what we *are*. It means to be persons who are shaped—all the way through—by the patterns of God's life and kingdom.

Perhaps a helpful analogy would be the experience of human culture. Culture is a network of values, qualities, and priorities that shape the patterns of life in that culture. We don't even think about it most of the time. We just reflect it.

I discovered this in a new way some years ago while serving in Europe. At that time, the social unrest in Eastern Europe that would eventually redraw the political map of

Europe was just beginning. Our church in West Germany helped two refugees, giving them shelter and support in a transitional time as they worked on permanent relocation to the United States. As the host pastor, I had the opportunity to introduce them to a new world. The time I spent with them was a rich learning experience as I observed western culture in a new way through their eyes as they encountered it for the first time.

One of the insights was a fresh vision of Americans. One of our congregations was made up of Americans. There was also a large military community in our area, allowing the Europeans to come into extensive contact with Americans. One day Robert, one of the refugees, commented on his amazement and admiration for how Americans walk. I have to confess that I had never considered the idea that there was a distinctive American "walk," so I pressed him to explain what he meant. What captivated him, he explained, was the boldness and freedom with which Americans walk. Their heads are up, looking boldly ahead, unafraid to look you in the eye. And, he explained further, Americans walk as if they expect to be able to go wherever they want to go—no tentativeness, no uncertainty, no fear. They walk like people accustomed to generous freedom.

Now, this isn't a story about glorifying Americans (as much as I appreciate them). We have a generous list of flaws and limitations. But I did come away from that conversation with a new awareness of how our sense of the world and our place in it could even shape the way we walk. That's culture. It is a sense of identity, values, purpose, and place in the world that shapes how we live.

Kingdom Christians are persons shaped by God's life until their most basic sense of identity, values, purpose, and place in the world reflect that citizenship. In how we "walk," we reflect and express who we are—and whose we are.

THE HEART OF THE MATTER

The heart of the matter is . . . the heart. It is out of the heart that our deepest self emerges. Whoever we are *there* will ultimately determine how we live. Peter recognizes the importance of this as he calls Christians to kingdom living. He describes a changed reality for his readers that goes all the way to the heart. Their obedience to God—submission to His Lordship—resulted in a transformation. Peter describes it as purifying. Something radical and decisive has happened. As a result of that purifying transformation, their *hearts* are changed. They are able to love their brothers and sisters in the faith in a new way—not feigned or superficially, but sincerely.

Because that is true, Peter calls them to "love one another deeply, from the heart" (1 Peter 1:22*b*). What he describes is a loving response that is undivided, a way of living that is total in its commitment to the other, emerging from a heart that has been changed to be able to do just that. Live from the center, he is telling them, from the heart.

Kingdom citizenship is formed from the inside-out. The kind of life Peter is writing about begins at the center. If the heart can be changed, then the rest of our lives can be successfully changed too. When we try to change from the outside-in, we are destined for frustration and failure. Christianity that takes the form of legalism or rigorous rules for living inevitably misses the point.

You can restrain or subdue a wild animal—for a while and with difficulty. Your relationship with the captive animal will be adversarial, lived out in a constant struggle for control. A momentary lapse of attention or discipline can result in a break to freedom. As long as that animal is wild, its captivity is only tentative, and probably temporary. You have restrained its actions, but the heart is still wild.

God doesn't want that kind of captive citizens in His

kingdom. Kingdom citizenship is not about effectively re-
straining ourselves from doing what we really want to do. It
is being changed to *desire* the life God offers. This is the log-
ic behind Augustine's easily misunderstood dictum, "Love
God and do what you want." The heart is the key. Change in
the life begins in the heart. Obedience to God, submission
to His kingdom, results in a definitive transformation—
a purification—that enables us to *want* to live in a new
way. We are made new citizens of the Kingdom—from the
inside-out.

WORKING IT OUT

Kingdom citizenship begins from the inside-out. However, what we *do* both expresses and shapes who we are. It
isn't a matter of either/or for the life of the Kingdom, but
both/and. If a Christianity of external rules misses the point,
we should also note that a Christianity that claims to be a
matter of the heart but doesn't include the life we live *also*
misses the point.

Integrity is a description of consistency. All of the parts
are in harmony; they reflect the same values or character.
Kingdom citizens have integrity. Their hearts and their lives
are shaped by the same identity, values, and purpose. Citizens
of God's kingdom *act* like citizens of the Kingdom. The heart
and the life can't be separated. That's why Peter moves from
the heart to patterns of living. *Because* our hearts are changed,
we *must* change our habits, attitudes, and behaviors.

When we "love deeply from a pure heart," we are compelled to "rid ourselves" of attitudes and actions that are not
loving. The language that Peter uses is pretty emphatic, but it's
not about law. It is the natural action of a recentered life. Have
you ever observed (or experienced yourself) someone who discovered that his or her clothes had some kind of insect or unpleasant infestation? It doesn't take long to "rid ourselves" of
that clothing. And we don't need much encouragement!

Kingdom citizens begin to "see" themselves and their lives in a new way. Attitudes, behaviors, and actions are revealed in a new light. Patterns and behaviors that had been pleasant and agreeable now increasingly appear distasteful and inappropriate. A changed heart calls for a changed life.

This doesn't mean that changed living simply "happens" or that intentional effort and purposeful spiritual discipline are unnecessary. Settled attitudes, behaviors, and habits resist change, and reformation requires real effort. Still, a changed heart means that we approach disciplined formation differently. It is not a willful exertion of discipline to restrain us, to impose patterns of action against our will. It is a purposeful reordering of our habits, patterns, and behaviors in harmony or consistent with the character of life we desire. It is the intentional patterning of our lives from the inside-out.

Spiritual discipline and reordering life patterns still requires effort and can be hard work. But it is no longer work that is at odds with the heart of who we are and want to be. It is not an attempt to "force" us to be what we should be. It is the labor of really becoming what we *want* to be.

WHEN THE CURTAIN FALLS

I love Disney World. What an amazing place! Beautiful buildings and landscaping. Dramatic and colorful rides and magical places. I especially enjoy the characters. At any moment you might encounter a favorite cartoon character. What fun! It really is a Magic Kingdom.

But when the day ends and the park closes, the Magic Kingdom becomes an empty façade. The characters take off their costumes and resume their lives as real people. Of course, you never see them. Part of the "magic" of that kingdom is protected by the care they take to be sure you never see the characters as they really are. They work hard to protect the illusion.

Some folks think that Christianity is like the Magic

Kingdom. We work hard to keep up the image—until the "curtain falls." We expend our best effort to keep up the role while we are in public view. We try not to change out of our holy character costumes until we are out of sight. Only then can we relax and really be ourselves!

God's kingdom is more than a good show. Citizenship in God's kingdom means more than a role we play or a way that we "perform." Citizenship in God's kingdom defines us—from the inside-out. We can't put it on or take it off because it describes who we are—all the way through.

If you peek in on God's kingdom and His people "after hours," you will see the same things you have seen during "business hours." That is certainly not to say that kingdom citizens are perfect 24/7. Certainly not! But it does mean that who they are and how they live is shaped and measured —all the time—by that citizenship.

ALL OF THIS FOR NOTHING?

Let's return to our confused caregiver and her frustrated question. Was the compassionate service of all those years for nothing? Did her discovery of God's grace mean that next week she could be free of this unpleasant servant task?

I think the right answer is actually yes—and no. While it is not my prerogative (thankfully!) to judge the merits of her service, it is true that God wants more than external acts of mercy. His intention is not for kingdom citizens to do good deeds "against their will." What she did may have been noble, even praiseworthy, but it wasn't really a model for kingdom life. Her troubled response exposed her actions as coming from a sense of duty or obligation rather than emerging from the heart.

On the other hand, the discovery of God's grace and the reality of a changed heart wouldn't mean the end of her servanthood—in this or other ways. To be a citizen of the Kingdom is to be changed—from the inside-out—to reflect the character of God's life. Who we are and what we do is shaped by that changed identity—that transformed heart. Serving those who need help is just the kind of thing that God does. So, it is just the kind of thing that God's kingdom-people do. How we "walk" emerges from who we are and what we are becoming—from the inside-out.

Kingdom Christians should really look like "foreigners." Because we are. Our citizenship—our hearts—really belong to another kingdom, another lordship, than the one we are living in. The curiosities of our behavior, the strange ordering of our priorities, the different patterns of living, all emerge out of that citizenship—that shapes us from the inside-out. We live here; but we belong to another kingdom. And that makes all the difference.

Scripture Cited: Leviticus 11:45; 1 Peter 1:15-16, 22

About the Author: Dr. Leth is chair of the department of religion and philosophy at Olivet Nazarene University, Bourbonnais, Illinois.

TRUTH TO REMEMBER

Kingdom Christians hear and obey
God's calling in life.

ANSWER GOD'S CALL

BY JEANETTE GARDNER LITTLETON

Len has been a youth minister in various churches over the past 20 years. For his most recent position, he moved his family halfway across the country and worked full-time as a church's youth minister for nearly a year at only a part-time salary and no insurance while the church got their budget issues figured out. Then, as they promised, the church hired him full-time with the appropriate salary and benefits. Len thought everything was going great. His ministry was flourishing. But now, after Len has officially been on the full-time church staff for less than a year, the church has asked him to leave. They've decided they should have hired someone who is not just a veteran in youth ministry but also has more experience in children's ministries.

This is not the first time this sort of thing has happened to Len. Though most of his career has been with flourishing youth ministries, his last three youth pastor positions have ended unexpectedly and painfully. It's enough to make many people doubt that they were in the right field, but Len has plugged on, knowing God has called him.

Yet now, with his growing family to feed, and the past three churches honestly not treating Len and his family right, Len is looking at returning to his previous career in the military.

"I still know I'm called," he says. "God has called me, as

a Christian, to minister—whether it's in a professional ministry capacity or not. Whether it's in youth ministry or the military."

EVERY BELIEVER IS CALLED

Len has felt the calling to be a youth minister for years. However, more than being called *to* a specific area, he knows that God has given him a calling to serve Him.

Like Len, every Christian has received a calling—a calling to be set apart from others in the world who don't know God. A calling to serve God, and live for Him, and with an intrinsic consciousness of a life beyond the here and now.

One of the first times in the Bible where we read about God's call to individuals is in Genesis 12. Abram, later known as Abraham, was 75 years old when he heard God's call. And what a call it was! "The LORD had said to Abram, 'Leave your country, your people and your father's household and go to the land I will show you.' . . . So Abram left, as the LORD had told him" (vv. 1, 4).

Have you noticed anything odd about that calling? God told Abram to "go" but didn't tell him where he was supposed to go. That would be like being invited to an event, but not told the location. Like the host saying, "Just leave your house and start out, and when you're where you're supposed to be, I'll call you on your cell phone and let you know."

Most of us would have been hounding God with questions: "But *where* am I supposed to go? I can't just set out without knowing where I'm going. Can't You be more organized than that? Can we get some clues here?"

But not Abram. He just followed God's directions and left. Abraham is often cited as an example of faith because he trusted God with the life of his son, Isaac (see Genesis 22). Actually, he was an example of faith way before that. He's an example of faith to us here, from the time we first read about him in Scripture.

Abram could answer God's call because he trusted God. He had faith that God would not lead him to death but to more abundant life, as He promised.

As we answer God's call, we, too, must display faith. As with Abram, sometimes God isn't specific. Sometimes He just tells us to pack up and head out, but doesn't tell where we'll end up. It's never easy to head out when we don't know where we're going, but God will reward our faith, just as He promised to reward Abram (vv. 2-3).

PLACES WE NEVER EXPECTED

God was a little more specific when He called Moses. Exodus 2:25 tells us, "God looked on the Israelites and was concerned about them." The Israelites, the descendants God had promised Abram in Genesis 5:2-3, were living as slaves to the Egyptians. And their living conditions kept getting worse. God heard their pleas and remembered His promise to bless Abram's descendants, so He acted. We don't know exactly how He approached Abram, but He was a bit more dramatic with Moses. He drew Moses' attention with a burning bush. Then, when He called Moses' name, Moses immediately responded.

God was a little more explicit than He'd been with Abram. He told Moses exactly what He wanted Him to do (see Exodus 3—4). Moses wasn't as eager to answer the call as Abram had been. "What if they don't listen?" he asked (see 4:1). He parried a few more questions about his abilities to do the job, then finally said, "O Lord, please send some-one else to do it" (4:13).

One of my spiritual mentors used to tell the story this way: "God called Moses to lead the Israelites out of Egypt and into the Promised Land. Moses told him, 'Lord, I can't do that!' God said, 'I know you can't. Now get going!'"

Moses was so wrapped up in his inabilities that he didn't focus on God's abilities.

God may call us to do great things, or He may call us to do mundane things in great ways. Either way, when He calls us, we can't make a checklist and say, "Well, I can certainly do this and this and this, but I don't have the ability to do that or that."

God wasn't happy about Moses' response (see 4:14). It looks in this scripture as if calling Aaron to be the spokesperson for Moses was God's compromise with Moses, not God's original, best plan. Who knows what would have happened if Moses had just answered, "Sure," with the faith that Abram had? Perhaps if Moses hadn't argued with his call, he would have been a stronger leader without Aaron, and Aaron wouldn't have had the haughtiness, or whatever it was, to help the Israelites make idols when Moses met with God on the mountain (see Exodus 32:1-7). Who knows?

When God calls us, we can't focus on our inabilities. Rather, we must focus on God and His abilities. God's call usually stretches us in some way or another. That's where faith comes in, and that's where we see God's strength and power and miracles—when He infuses ordinary humans with the ability to do extraordinary things way outside of their normal capacities. Then the people who are watching our lives know it's God working through us. God's calling can take us way beyond where we would normally go, to places we never expected.

Perhaps sometimes God doesn't tell us where He's leading us because, like Moses, we might get scared and be tempted to run or to not answer the call!

GOD'S CALLING IS NOT TROUBLE-FREE

If God calls us and empowers us, if He's in charge, the living out of that call should be easy, right?

Moses would certainly disagree! All of his years of leading the Israelites to the Promised Land were filled with headaches.

Like Moses, Paul experienced a dramatic call from the Lord. He hated believers and was immersed in persecuting them. In fact, he was on his way to Damascus for the sole purpose of ferreting out the Christians and legally prosecuting them when he heard Jesus calling to him (see Acts 9:1-6).

From that point on, Paul was as zealous in spreading the gospel of Jesus Christ as he'd been in trying to squelch it. God's call took Paul to some rough places. God's call landed him in jail at different times. In his pursuit of God's call, Paul even ended up shipwrecked. At other times, the call led him to defend himself in court. Paul seemed to go from one stressful situation to the next, and all of it was a response of his answering God's call.

Our friend Len, whom we mentioned at the beginning of the chapter, can relate. Though Len answered God's call into the youth ministry, it wasn't easy sailing from there. Even when Len's ministry to teens was flourishing, he still had to deal with other adults in the church. He still had to deal with humans, who, in their unsanctified state can let sin rule in their lives, and who, even in the sanctified state, can certainly make mistakes in judgment that hurt others.

Most of us who answer God's call, like Len, at some point or another, face pain and trouble in the midst of trying to live out God's call. Sometimes, unfortunately, it comes from other well-meaning (or not so well-meaning) people in the church. Sometimes, as with Paul, we get whammied from those outside of the church.

Sometimes the trouble comes from thoughtlessness or other people's lack of faith, like the Israelites who kept doubting God. At other times, the trouble we encounter is just part of life. And sometimes it's direct spiritual warfare. After all, if the spiritual world is real—and Christians believe it is—then we're involved in something that goes beyond the material world. Paul reminded us in Ephesians that "our struggle is not against flesh and blood, but against the rulers, against the authorities, against the powers of this dark world and against the spiritual forces of evil in the heavenly realm" (6:12).

So when we answer God's call, we can expect to face the tough stuff of life. At those times, Paul encourages us to find our strength in God and to equip ourselves spiritually for the attack.

THE CALL REQUIRES PERSISTENCE

When we answer God's call, we're automatically set apart from others. We become different from the general populace on earth without even trying. Peter points out, "But you are a chosen people, a royal priesthood, a holy nation, a people belonging to God, that you may declare the praises of him who called you out of darkness into his wonderful light" (1 Peter 2:9).

Some versions of this scripture say we're a "peculiar" people. Those versions highlight the point that we're different from the rest of the world. At times, people in the world are not going to know what to make of us. At best, when they see God in our lives, they may approve and be drawn to know God themselves. At other times, they may think we're odd but somewhat harmless. In seemingly worst-case scenarios, they will hate us for those differences.

So, what are we supposed to do?

People who are pursuing the call need to have the attitude that Texas drivers have. I love visiting Texas, and have spent much time north of Dallas. One thing that I'm always reminded of when I drive the country highways leading into Dallas is that Texans don't let other people slow them down when they're on a mission.

Going to turn left on a road that only has one lane in each direction? Fine. While you're sitting and waiting for the traffic to clear so you can turn, a true Texas driver won't sit patiently behind you, waiting for you to get out of his way. That doesn't mean he'll sit there and impatiently honk at

you either. No siree. He won't even slow down. He'll just
zoom around you on the shoulder of the road.

You can do what you want, but he's going to keep on
heading to his destination. That doesn't mean Texans can't
be kind drivers, I've learned. They're just goal-oriented when
they're on the road.

When we're answering God's call, we need to have that
Texas mind-set: we must pursue that direction without letting others slow us down. We can't let those turning in other
directions hinder our goals or our destination.

That's one of the things I admire about Len. Knowing
the details of the situations Len has faced, I'd be having
some pity parties and be doubting my call if I were in Len's
shoes. But Len has the persistence to keep going. Like Paul,
he forgets what's behind in his focus to "press on toward the
goal to win the prize for which God has called me heavenward in Christ Jesus" (Philippians 3:14).

GOD'S CALL IS FLUID

God's call in a Christian's life is unchangeable. After
calling us, He will never "uncall" us. He will never say, "OK,
your job's done. Go back to being who you were and doing
what you want to do." When He calls us, it's a permanent
call. He wants us to be set apart, chosen, and following Him
for the rest of our earthly lives and beyond.

Still, God's call may not be permanent in how it's lived
out.

When God originally called Moses, he focused on telling Moses to lead His people out of Egypt. Though He
mentioned the part that ended up being lifelong for Moses
—leading them into the Promised Land—God focused on
the first part of the call: leading the Israelites out of Egypt.

So many years ago, Len felt God calling Him to be a
youth leader. Now Len's discovering that God's call may lead
him in another direction. And even if God leads Len into

the military again, in another 2, 10, or 20 years, His call may segue Len into another platform for living out that call.

That's one of the beauties of Christianity. Life changes quicker than a seascape. The waves constantly roll in and out. The shoreline in our lives subtly adapts all the time. Whether the waves are calm or churning, God's call endures. We can count on the stability of that, though at times it takes a different shape or focus as part of our ever-changing lives.

As Abram found, God doesn't give us a life-map, telling us exactly where God's call is going to take us and when. God just calls us to move, to follow Him. He may lead us to Canaan for a few years. Then famine may hit, and He may lead us to live out that call in Egypt for a while (see Genesis 12:10). Then He may lead us back to Canaan, where we encounter strife with members of our own physical or spiritual family (see Genesis 13). Later His call may lead us to rescue those very family members who gave us such a hard time (see Genesis 14). At times, His calling may seem to focus on our being physically active; at other times, our call may be to quietly watch and pray. Sometimes God may bring obvious, fruitful results and blessings as a result of our following His call. At other times, like Abraham waiting 25 years for that son, God may seem slow in fulfilling His promises because we don't know His purposes.

In John 6, many of Jesus' followers left him because he was telling them tough things to hear (see v. 66). Jesus turned to His disciples and asked if they were going to leave Him too. Peter answered, "Lord, to whom shall we go? You have the words of eternal life" (v. 68).

God's call may lead us into sunshine, or into forays of darkness. But at all times, may we have the grace to respond, as Peter did, "Who else can we follow? You have the Words of Life."

Scripture Cited: Genesis 12:1, 4; Exodus 2:25; 4:13; John 6:68; Ephesians 6:12; Philippians 3:14; 1 Peter 2:9

About the Author: Jeannette Littleton is a freelance writer, who lives in Gladstone, Missouri, with her husband, Mark, and their children.

TRUTH TO REMEMBER

Kingdom Christians are concerned with the same issues as God.

10

SHARE GOD'S CONCERNS

BY JOHN HAY JR.

A great-grandmother in her early 80s, Helen was living safely in a suburban community. Through her holiness heritage, she had learned to take seriously the call to a holy life. For Helen, that included daily prayer and Bible reading, to be sure, but also study and service. She loved to read challenging books; she frequently shared large-print editions of spiritual classics with friends. When she learned at her local church that help was needed in a new compassionate ministry in the inner city, she readily volunteered.

Over her family's protests, Helen began to make the weekly drive from the suburbs into the heart of the city. There she would listen, pray, and counsel with families struggling in the grip of poverty. Helen, prim and proper, sitting across a table from a homeless man was a sight to behold. Her high heels and "church lady" clothes belied the spirit of compassion she shared with each person. Her encounters with hurting inner-city neighbors would be the focus of her prayers and concerned conversations for the rest of the week. When complimented about her exceptional service, Helen would emphatically defer, "I'm just doing what I think Jesus would do. If He were here, He would be serving the poor." Before her health failed when she was 88, Helen had counseled with hundreds of inner-city neighbors over a seven-year span. Before she died, she told her family that serving the poor brought her the most joy in life.

What makes it seem "normal" for a woman in her 80s to choose to volunteer to assist the poor? What causes her to routinely leave the relative safety of her suburban world to take "unnecessary risks" in the inner-city? What prompts a Christian to step out of his enclave of security to begin to defend the rights of unjustly treated people? What moves a believer to care less for her personal financial portfolio than for the fact that her corporate employer is paying unlivable wages to overseas laborers working long hours in unsafe conditions? What readily draws some earnest Christians beyond their comfort zones and across cultural lines through giving, serving, and sacrificing for the sake of healing hurting people they may never directly meet?

AN ANCIENT MESSAGE

Somewhere along her Christian journey, Helen began to recognize that she should be concerned about things over which God is concerned. She discovered that the call to be Christlike was neither completed at conversion nor fulfilled within the walls of the church. The challenge to "be imitators of God" (Ephesians 5:1) was taken with a literal frankness that propelled her to attempt to "live a life of love, just as Christ loved us and gave himself up for us as a fragrant offering and sacrifice to God" (v. 2). For Helen, and for many others like her, the imitation of Christ means discovering what God is concerned about and simply—profoundly—aligning one's witness and service with those concerns. Having become convinced that one of God's primary concerns is poverty, it was "normal" for Helen to respond to the call for help and spend her last years in joyful service to the poor.

It is doubtful that Helen would have known the profound level of God's concern for the poor had she not been a persistent Bible reader and lover of good Christian literature.

Concern for issues, such as poverty, usually takes a backseat to calls to personal salvation and other interests in local congregational conversation. But active Bible readers discover that God's passionate concern for the poor pervades the Old and New Testaments.

Moses called upon the Israelites to always remember, along with God's deliverance, their own slavery in Egypt. They were to reflect God's graciousness in their concern for strangers, aliens, and the poor in their midst. Deuteronomy 15:7-8 captures the essence of many covenant calls to relieve the poor: "Do not be hardhearted or tightfisted toward your poor brother. Rather be open-handed and freely lend him whatever he needs." Why remember and relieve the poor? Because "we were slaves of Pharaoh in Egypt, but the LORD brought us out of Egypt with a mighty hand" (Deuteronomy 6:21). As God had been concerned for them in their plight, so the Israelites were to be concerned for others caught in the grip of slavery and poverty.

Jesus focused His attention on the poor from the outset of His public service (see Luke 4:16-21). When He saw them, "he had compassion on them, because they were harassed and helpless, like sheep without a shepherd" (Matthew 9:36). He called them "blessed" (Luke 6:20) and made it clear that disregarding "the least of these" would exclude one from eternal fellowship (see Matthew 25:31-46). When asked to give evidence that He was the authentic Messiah, Jesus simply stated: "The blind receive sight, the lame walk, those who have leprosy are cured, the deaf hear, the dead are raised, and the good news is preached to the poor" (Matthew 11:5).

In the power of the Holy Spirit, the Early Church continued and extended Jesus' concern for the poor. After Pentecost, believers sold possessions and goods to relieve those in need (see Acts 2:45). Remembering the poor in Jerusalem through offerings received among the Gentile churches is a constant throughout the apostle Paul's travels and ministry.

Beyond New Testament days, the Church continued to be the first friend, protector, and defender of the poor, disinherited, stranger, foreigner, diseased, and outcast. For these, the door was always and especially open. Ancient Christians cared for the poor, not in order to be noted as exceptional or charitable, but because in doing so they believed they were reflecting the very character and concern of God.

FAITH IN ACTION

A few years ago, a young evangelical minister cut out of his Bible all passages referring to poverty and injustice. He found that that Bible literally fell apart in his hands when these many references were removed. In the years since, Jim Wallis has given his life to speak, write, teach, and act for these biblical concerns that others have readily set aside, subdued, or discarded as unimportant to the evangelical Christian witness.

Throughout Christian history, people who read the Bible for themselves get both a wide-angle and close-up view of what concerns God. Often these people have taken God's primary interests for individuals and communities at face value and tried to authentically reflect them in their lives. While onlookers are sometimes startled at their so-called "extreme" steps to care for the destitute, alleviate poverty, reconcile "impossible" enemies, or intervene to break the grip of injustice, these Bible-believing people act in the faith that they are doing nothing out of the ordinary, or at least nothing out of what would be ordinary for God.

Recently, after reading Matthew 25, a Christian woman living in suburban Indianapolis felt like she should help homeless neighbors. Leann was concerned about those who face bitter cold at night. She ran across a web site describing how simple sleeping bags could be made using scraps of fabric. No seamstress, Leann bought a sewing machine at a garage sale, taught herself to sew, and called upon friends to give her their old fabric and blankets. Before long, Leann was sewing 25 sleeping bags a month. The randomly colorful patchwork bags, affectionately called "ugly quilts," were rolled up and tied with equally ugly men's ties. She also sewed a pocket on each ugly quilt and slipped in a paperback Bible. Each month now, Leann delivers a fresh supply of "ugly quilts" to homeless shelters in the inner city. "I'm just doing what I can; what I think Jesus would have me do," she says of this service.

A PROPHETIC VOICE

Closely reading the Bible, one would eventually begin to notice passages that describe a level of God's concern that moves considerably *beyond* relief of the poor. For instance, one would find in Isaiah 58 a clarion call to address the *causes* of poverty and *sources* of injustice. On the surface, people seem to be doing the right religious things; they appear to be spiritually sincere:

"For day after day they seek me out;
they seem eager to know my ways,
as if they were a nation that does what is right
and has not forsaken the commands of its God.
They ask me for just decisions
and seem eager for God to come near them.
'Why have we fasted,' they say,
'and you have not seen it?
Why have we humbled ourselves,
and you have not noticed?'" (Isaiah 58:2-3a).

But at the same time the congregation is lauding their traditional values and praying for revival in the land, they are not really concerned about what God is concerned about. There is a disconnect between their religious desires and any sense of justice in the marketplace and employment relationships. The prophecy exposes this spiritual schizophrenia:

"Yet on the day of your fasting, you do as you please

and exploit all your workers.
Your fasting ends in quarreling and strife,
and in striking each other with wicked fists.
You cannot fast as you do today
and expect your voice to be heard on high" (Isaiah
58:3*b*-4).

As the prophecy continues, God makes clear that spiritual disciplines that are not accompanied by heart-brokenness for how people are treated in the larger society are pointless. Dutiful devotions and faithful attendance in worship that do not result in challenge and change in unjust economic and social structures miss the point entirely. God's glory is scandalized by words of worship that do not really carry over into actions that reflect God's concern in day-to-day conflicts, struggles, and structures in which we live. So, what is God concerned about? What is the kind of fasting that will get God's attention? What is the way to revival in the land? The Word of God declares:
"Is not this the kind of fasting I have chosen:
to loose the chains of injustice
and untie the cords of the yoke,
to set the oppressed free
and break every yoke?
Is it not to share your food with the hungry
and to provide the poor wanderer with shelter—
when you see the naked, to clothe him,
and not to turn away from your own flesh and blood?"
(Isaiah 58:6-7).

These are not hard social concepts to understand. These are not obscure commands. They are direct, clear, and eminently doable. And they reflect in one fell swoop much of what God tries repeatedly to convey through the voices of many prophets: *Relief and charity are important and necessary, but they are no substitute for structural or systemic justice.*
Roughly translated into today's socioeconomic environment, "systemic justice" means such things as: establishing fair hir-

ing practices, providing livable wages to all workers, ending human exploitation, checking unlimited greed, challenging gross inequities, balancing individual will with community good, and working together for life-giving purposes more important than individual stockholders' maximum quarterly dividends.

The problem is not in the transmission or understanding of God's concern; the problem lies in Isaiah 58's challenge to personal lifestyles, financial portfolios, consumer habits, employment practices, national policies, and global economic strategies. God's concern is quite understandable. However, given our willing complicity in a complex set of economic and social practices that are now woven into the web of a global economy, change is difficult. Still, difficult or not, change is necessary—if we are to be kingdom Christians who reflect God's concern in a world that does not.

Some kingdom Christians, using their influence in corporations, governments, or communities, may be called upon to challenge and address one or more of these structural sins at a broad-based level. They may assist their respective organizations to explore horizons that take a longer, wider view of the impact of corporate or community norms, policies, and practices on the poor or foreign laborers. Other kingdom Christians may participate in dismantling unjust practices and heralding Kingdom-affirming policies by their personal choices in the marketplace, or by joining with others in collectively calling for fair practices and responsible corporate behavior. Either way, the challenge is likely to be long, victories slow, and the struggle continuous.

Calling for justice and compassion in entrenched organizational patterns or accepted social norms is the arena of spiritual warfare. This "struggle is not against flesh and blood, but against the rulers, against the authorities, against the powers of this dark world and against the spiritual forces of evil" (Ephesians 6:12). Kingdom Christians understand the difficulty of this struggle. Still, they do not shrink back

or write the world off or withdraw into illusory subcultures.
In the face of spiritual strongholds and structural injustice,
Jesus taught His disciples to dare to pray—and live as the
answer with their lives—"Your kingdom come, your will be
done on earth as it is in heaven" (Matthew 6:10).

For those who take God's concerns in Isaiah 58 seriously and attempt to work them into their relationships and
lifestyle, God's Word is quite promising:

Then your light will break forth like the dawn,
and your healing will quickly appear;
then your righteousness will go before you,
and the glory of the LORD will be your rear guard.
Then you will call, and the LORD will answer;
you will cry for help, and he will say: Here am I.
If you do away with the yoke of oppression,
with the pointing finger and malicious talk,
and if you spend yourselves in behalf of the hungry
and satisfy the needs of the oppressed,
then your light will rise in the darkness,
and your night will become like the noonday (Isaiah
58:8-10).

TAKING THE RISK

Revival results when we care as much for fairness in the
workplace as we do the favor of God. Revival results when
earnest, prayerful believers align their concerns with—and
put their lives on the line for—what concerns God.

Perhaps a warning label should be placed on the outside
of Bibles: "Caution: Consuming this product may radically
change your perception of Christian values, political priorities, attitudes toward enemies, investment strategies, and/or
career choices. Read at your own risk!" Of course, who dares
to calculate the risk of neither reading nor heeding for one-
self the Word of God? In the face of many influences and
voices claiming to be right or important or ultimate, king-

dom Christians learn to dwell on, listen to, and heed the Word of God through all and above all. As they do, they discover more and more about what really concerns God, and they find grace to share that concern with their neighbors and world.

Scripture Cited: Deuteronomy 6:21; 15:7-8; Isaiah 58:2-4, 6-10; Matthew 6:10; 9:36; 11:5; Luke 6:20; Ephesians 5:1-2; 6:12

About the Author: Dr. Hay is pastor of West Morris Street Free Methodist Church in Indianapolis.

TRUTH TO REMEMBER

Kingdom Christians spend their leisure time
in God-honoring ways.

11

GODLY TIME OFF

BY ELLEN COX

Have you ever been around someone with a serious hobby? I'm not speaking of the dabbler who just occasionally participates in an activity, but one who wholeheartedly is devoted to the pursuit of his or her fascination.

For instance, I like birds. I enjoy listening to their songs and even enjoy watching them when they land on my fence post to look for and eat the grass seed my husband lays out. My friend, however, is a devoted bird watcher. She's been a member of the Audubon Society, she's taken bird-watching outings with others who share her passion, and she's even started her own business selling supplies to those who want to develop this hobby. If you walked into my friend's house, there would be no mistaking her love for nature. Her love for these delicate and graceful creations is obvious and apparent to all. She is serious about birds, and it affects what she does. The same goes for the "serious Christian." A kingdom Christian's passion is going to affect his or her time off.

We can see the standard set for faith-altered lives in 1 Peter 1:15, where it says, "Be holy in everything you do, just as God . . . is holy" (NLT). Notice the all-inclusive "everything." How many times would we try to give just *some* things or try to give everything on only *some* days? Daunting task, I know, but one that must be undertaken if we are going to really live with God's kingdom at the forefront of our lives. This pursuit isn't easy, but the rewards are far greater than anything we can think or imagine.

TIME IN THE WORD

As in all things, we first want to look to Christ for the model of honoring God even in our time off. In Mark 6:31, Jesus and the disciples were so pressed in by their duties and the crowds they didn't even have time to eat. How many times do we get so busy with our jobs and responsibilities that we forget to "eat"? I've had many times, more times than I wish I had to admit, that I have chosen to do other things rather than take my daily nourishment of God's Bread. There have been times that if you could have had special glasses that allowed you to see my spiritual body, I must have looked emaciated indeed! Think about your day: how many times have you started your day with a good meal of God's Living Word, and felt better, had more energy, and generally just more equipped? Notice, I didn't say everything was great and trouble-free. As a matter of fact, the day held all of the same responsibilities and complications, you just felt better able to handle what came up. Making God's Word a part of your time off increases the benefits of the rest period you are taking. Just as diets have increased effectiveness with exercise, good sleep increases stamina, and practice increases our abilities at any endeavor, so reading God's Word makes the most of our days, no matter what they hold.

Isaiah 55:11 speaks of the effectiveness of God's Word. It says, "They [God's Words] don't return without doing everything I send them to do" (author's paraphrase). Second Timothy 3:16-17 lists the many ways God's Word is used by God to accomplish His work in us. He uses it to instruct, teach, correct, exemplify right living, and equip us for every job He asks us to do. If God's Word doesn't return empty-handed without finishing its task, then we have to place priority on spending time reading it.

I can't tell you how many times I have gone through periods of difficulty and doubt in my walk of faith, without my first place to go for help being my Bible. I would read books by great Christian authors; I would attend wonderful, uplifting seminars; and seek advice from great counselors in my church. They would give great words of wisdom, and then always end by claiming time spent every day in God's Word was the final and ultimate answer to my struggles. *Have a positive attitude? Great! I can do that! Forgive my neighbor? Done! Volunteer in service? Where do I sign up? Bible Study? Whoa! By the time I do all that thinking, forgiving, and volunteering, I'm tuckered out! Can't a gal get some rest? I know God's Word is important and all, but I'll get to it later, I just want to sit down and catch a second or two of this TV show.* Sound familiar? No, my thoughts may not have been that blatant, but my actions sure were. By not taking the time to really digest God's Word, I was stating, through action, the priority I placed on it.

That's my own story, but lest you think it's just my idea, look again at Christ's example. Many times Jesus demonstrated the importance of incorporating time spent with God alone. It helped to restore His energies, yes, but it also restored His focus. At the time of His greatest need before His greatest physical taxation, He was alone with God, surrendering His will and His very life. This causes us to ask, can real and healthy growth happen without proper "nutrition"?

TIME FOR THE SABBATH

God created the day of Sabbath for the purpose of taking a break from work. In Leviticus 19, God gave the Israelites His plan for showing the other nations that they were unique. His first statement echoes the 1 Peter passage. God demands Israel's imitation of His holiness in their personal conduct. At the top of that list is His requirement to "observe my Sabbaths" (v. 3). As a matter of fact, the first example of the importance of rest comes from God's first rest break in Genesis 2:2.

If keeping the Sabbath is a part of God's holiness, it must become something that is a priority for us as well. It is an integral part of the resting that we are to do. If serious mental deficiencies result from not sleeping, then consider keeping the Sabbath as the spiritual side of the coin. Jesus said the Sabbath was made for people. It's not only a day for honoring and worshiping God; it was made and instituted for our benefit. There is a reason we are asked to not give up the practice of meeting together with other believers: It provides the accountability, teaching, and community that we need to walk this narrow path.

We might be able to get by on five or six hours of sleep a night, but it catches up with us, and doesn't maintain our health as effectively. So it is with the Sabbath. We just don't maintain as healthy a spiritual body when we deprive it of that time spent with other believers. It might be silly to ask someone, "Do you take time to sleep at night?" Yet, the question still has to be asked in the spiritual context. "Do you take time for the Sabbath?" How many times is that answer "No"? We just might have some very sleepy drivers on the eternal highway!

TIME FOR OUTREACH

Jesus also took many opportunities to take a break from public ministry. In Mark 10, He stopped his duties to play with and bless children (see vv. 13-16).

I have many lists of things to do and errands to run, so much so that the list seems endless at times. I generally have to force myself to set aside those things and make time to play with my children, do a craft, play "chase me" in the yard, even watch a movie with them. They call it "movie with Mommy," and it's one of their favorite activities. I must confess, it's one of my favorites too. It is a solid block of time that I can cuddle with my boys and, at the same time, monitor what they watch. They are blessed with my time, attention, and instruction; and I am blessed with their hugs, time to relax, and a better peek at what goes on in the active minds of my kids.

My sister-in-law is fortunate to live in a perpetually sunny and warm state. She loves to take advantage of it by taking her kids swimming regularly. She doesn't go in order to work on her tan, but to jump in and play with them, to build memories for them. When they get home from school, she'll stop what she's doing and pop popcorn. They will jump on her bed and take turns telling about their day. Sometimes it takes 15 minutes; sometimes they talk for an hour. After they are done, they have that feeling of closeness, and they are ready for the next part of their day.

My pastor's wife also loves to spend her free time with her grandchildren. She takes every opportunity she can to play with them and let them know just how special they are. Her granddaughters love to help with every aspect of mealtimes, from cooking, to setting the table, to cleaning up afterward. The children are blessed with her time and attention. They are validated, instructed, and feel the love of their grandmother in a practical way. How does this affect Jolene? She gets pure joy from the time spent with her grandchildren. She may be a little tired when they leave, but the joy and contentment she feels from investing herself in that time is immeasurable.

Although His ministry was all about sharing himself through service and sacrifice, even during His free time Jesus looked for ways to reach out to those who needed Him. He found ways to be a part of their lives. He didn't just stay in His comfortable space with His "church group"; He went to dinner with "sinners." After His day of public speaking and healing, instead of just lunching with His disciples, He went over to a tree and picked a certain person that everyone disdained and shared a meal with him. Jesus invested personal time in getting to know someone beyond the point that others had dismissed the person. He connected to someone who needed God. Jesus said He came to be a servant and to seek out those who were hurting and needed a touch from a Savior. If we are to be imitators of Christ—and we take that challenge seriously—should we not have the same goal?

My pastor is a wonderful and giving individual. He spends a lot of time tending to the needs of his congregation, both behind the pulpit and in front of it. A good majority of his time is given to the task of serving his congregation. Therefore, he guards the time with his family carefully. There was a time, however, that he was invited to a birthday dinner for a couple in his church whose son did not attend. While attending this dinner, my pastor had the opportunity to speak with both the son and his fiancé. While he did not share the gospel, he did share his time and love for them. He began the foundation for a relationship that could give him greater opportunity to not only share the gospel verbally but through his life and actions as well. He could have chosen to reject the invitation and taken his wife to dinner, just the two of them. Instead, he dined with others. He still benefited from the time off, but he also connected to someone who, through prayer and friendship, could be added to the Kingdom.

When my grandfather was a pastor of a church in Colorado Springs, he had a young couple who gave birth to twins. Most young couples back in those days didn't have a washer and dryer, and babies' diapers were cloth. Can you imagine how many cloth diapers twins could go through? My grandmother told the young, harried mother that she would launder all the babies' diapers. Every day my grandmother went over to their house, gathered all the diapers, took them home and washed, dried, and took them back folded and ready to use. She didn't have to do that. Can you imagine what that use of her free time did, not just for the couple, but the couples' neighbors? Would you be interested in hearing the gospel from someone who would put her faith into action that way?

TIME FOR HOBBIES

So if we are in God's Word, we are meeting with other believers regularly, and we look for opportunities to incorporate our leisure time with reaching out to others with Christ's love, what can we do with all of our other free time? How does our commitment to Christ affect our hobbies and our activities?

I'm a movie buff. I've been consulted about movie trivia when a friend was debating with someone about some point of a film. His first choice to solve the debate was to call me with the question. I was able to give him the correct answer before he even finished the question. My beliefs, however, limit my knowledge base because I have purposed to not watch something that Jesus would not sit down and watch with me. I have another friend who enjoys reading, but his commitment to God leads his choices of what he reads. Another friend takes road trips whenever possible. The things he does on these trips is first filtered through his convictions of giving everything over to God and to what is pleasing to Him.

TIME FOR JESUS

It is plain that we are trying to imitate a holiness lifestyle that invades every part of our life. If Jesus is the vine and we are the branches, does the fruit we bear resemble the plant? Jesus said a tree is identified by the fruit it produces. Likewise our life resembles His if we really believe God and are letting that passion for the things of God affect the kinds of things we do during our times of rest.

Father Pedro Arrupe was considered a very influential leader in the Roman Catholic Church, as well as beloved for his heart for service. His is an interesting story, one worth reading. However, for time's sake, I'll abbreviate it. Pedro

Arrupe started out in medicine. During his training, he met God in a real way, and his plans changed. He had such a love for God that he gave up his medical pursuits and dedicated his life to serving the God he loved by serving His people. He passionately served people for God's sake, until a stroke took his ability to speak or even move. He then dedicated the rest of his life to prayer and intercession on others' behalf. He understood well what having a life-changing relationship with God could do. One of his quotes sums up what I've been saying. He said, "Nothing is more practical than finding God, than falling in love in a quite absolute way. What you are in love with, what seizes your imagination, will affect everything. It will decide what will get you out of bed in the morning, what you will do with your evening, how you spend your weekends, what you read, whom you know, what breaks your heart, and what amazes you with joy and gratitude. Fall in love, stay in love, and it will decide everything."*

What has seized our heart? God's love changes things. Period. It changes water into wine, it changes a small lunch into a feast for a multitude, it changes the lame into walkers, the blind into seers, and it brings the dead new life. That kind of changing love changes our focus too. Fall in love with God, seek Him in everything. Follow the admonition of Paul in Colossians 3:1-2, 17: "Set your sights on the realities of heaven. . . . Let heaven fill your thoughts. Do not think only about things down here on earth. . . . And whatever you do or say, let it be as a representative of the Lord Jesus" (NLT).

Look at the status of our branches. We are grafted onto the heavenly vine. Are we bearing the fruit heaven produces? Does our tree look like it belongs in the Kingdom? Does our time off reflect the influence of the Savior? No greater endeavor can be undertaken than to dedicate everything, even our free time, to seeking to honor the One who created our time.

Notes:

*Encyclopedia Britannica Online, <britannica.com/ebi/article -9309937>

Scripture Cited: Leviticus 19:3; Isaiah 55:11; Colossians 3:1-2, 17; 1 Peter 1:15

About the Author: Ellen Cox is a freelance writer living with her family in Topeka, Kansas.

TRUTH TO REMEMBER

Kingdom Christians actively serve God
in many ways.

12

ACTIVE SERVICE

BY DAVID W. HOLDREN

It's buried somewhere in an unpacked box from the last big move. It was one of the more painful research articles I came across during some graduate studies at a secular university. It was simply titled, "The Good Samaritan Study." It left me weak with disappointment and embarrassed that it was probably descriptive of a sad reality.

It was from a social psychology research magazine, which addresses how people function in social settings. In this case, the subjects being studied were seminary students, young people preparing for Christian ministry. The object of the study was to see how beliefs impacted behavior.

Each student was scheduled to deliver a message on the New Testament story of the Good Samaritan from Luke 10:25-37. Some of the control factors in the research included having the students take a very specific route to their speaking engagement, and encountering en route a person who was in fairly obvious distress. Although the subject in need was not menacing, there was nonetheless a risk factor in stopping to help.

One third of the seminary students were sent so they would arrive in plenty of time, one third were sent to arrive just on time, and the last third were sent a bit late.

Even though the first third of the students had the time, the results of this study were that none of the seminary students stopped long enough to actually help the person in "need"—on their way to preach on the Good Samaritan! So, what were the implications? What a person claims to believe and even teaches others does not necessarily shape his or her own behavior.

I felt sick. It was a devastating indictment of Christians and Christianity. My first inclination was to cry "foul." But 20 years after reading that research piece, its demonstrated validity is what aggravates a wound in my heart. One of the biggest turnoffs to Christianity is not Christ; it is Christians!

Throughout my pastoral ministry, a dominant defense of those who avoided church was, "The church is full of hypocrites." In the early years, I responded to such comments with a sheepish nod of acknowledgement. Not anymore. Even with those who have been truly disappointed by the church scene, I now remind them that their workplace has plenty of hypocrites, and many of their friends make claims they don't support by their actions. And I hasten to add that the church is not a display case for perfect specimens, but a clinic for those in need. I *wanted* hypocrites in the church, I told them, because that way I knew there was always someone who needed what was being preached!

Also, I would confess to them that one of my greatest disappointments was that more of us who profess Christ do not better reflect Christ. Finally, I would offer my hunch that at some point in their past they were hurt by some church, some Christian, or even a pastor. Almost without fail, they softly answered in the affirmative. Even the rugged guys would admit to such unhealed experiences.

One of the most important priorities of our Christian life needs to be closing the gap between what we say we believe and how we live it, day by day.

The really good news is that many followers of Christ are indeed living lives of grace and love, and are terrific examples of life transformation. Millions of people in Christ's church are stellar examples of faith in action and are walking the talk. The problem is that they should be the norm, not the exception.

The exposure to the world of the child molestations by Catholic priests has made this very issue a headliner in recent years. This is not just a Catholic problem. Ministers and church layleaders of all stripes are losing the purity battle at an alarming rate. Yet, if we were to talk to 100 unchurched people and ask what they expected of the priests or pastors, they would not refer to better sermons or nicer confessional booths. They would expect us to live up to our calling!

What is the problem? Is our religion merely a lot of hot air? Is the talk of Christ living within us only a sentimental wish or a lame attempt to soften up God or impress others? Let's tackle this "reality" issue head-on.

First, we will review biblical expectations for a follower of Christ. Then we will attempt to identify the barriers we face in achieving our calling, and finally try to map out the pathway to living an authentic and contagious Christian life.

EXPECTATIONS

I mentioned earlier that even the unchurched folks expect Christians to live up to their name. What does the Bible say about how we live our lives? Let's begin with Jesus. "Not everyone who says to me, 'Lord, Lord,' will enter the kingdom of heaven, but only he who *does the will* of my Father who is in heaven" (Matthew 7:21, emphasis added).

Jesus follows that statement with the story about the person who builds a house on the rock and the other who builds on sand. When the storms came, guess which house collapsed? The difference was not just between rock and sand, but the *meaning* of "rock": putting Christ's words into practice! Active duty!

Jesus' half-brother James wrote one of the biblical books, and his total focus is on faith in action. Here is what he says: "Faith by itself, if it is not accompanied by action, is dead. . . . Show me your faith without deeds, and I will show you my faith by what I do. . . . Faith without deeds is useless" (James 2:17-18, 20). He goes on to say that faith and action work together, and faith is made complete by what we do. He also gives the comparison that just like the body without the spirit is dead, so faith without works is dead.

Some Christians interpret the Bible to teach that we cannot expect much transformation in the Christian life. They even suggest that God does not expect us to live righteous lives. When He looks at us, He sees the intervening Jesus, not us. Sounds good, and gives you and me some pretty big loopholes; but it's tough to drag that kind of teaching out of the Bible.

In contrast to that, along came our spiritual forefather John Wesley with what we now call his "optimism of grace." Wesley demonstrated that Scripture teaches that all people can be saved; all people can know that they are saved; and all people can be "saved to the uttermost," as he worded it.

God has high hopes for us all, and is willing to pay the price to help us achieve those hopes. So, what holds us back?

In his book, *The Divine Conspiracy,* Dallas Willard observes that in current North American Christianity, biblical teaching on personal salvation, with an emphasis on repentance and real transformation into the image of Christ, has been reduced to a simple divine pronouncement of forgiveness and a pronounced ticket to heaven. The myopic view of imputed righteousness and neglect to teach about the Holy Spirit's actual impartation of holiness has rendered evangelicalism powerless to bring about true Christian discipleship!*

Now, let's be specific about some of the behavior and character issues at stake. Although there are many, here are several highlighted by James: Faith . . .

    . . . doesn't give up under trials and pressure (1:3-12).
    . . . resists temptation and sin (1:13-15).
    . . . calls us to tame our tongues (1:19, 26; 3:1-12).
    . . . expects us to speak for the voiceless and protect the
        vulnerable (1:27).

. . . makes sacrifices (2:21).

. . . expects us to avoid spiritual pollution (4:7-8).

BARRIERS

Why do you suppose it is so common for those of us who ascribe allegiance to a holy God and claim to follow His Son to have so much trouble living up to our calling to be like our Lord? What are some of the key barriers?

Human Nature: The natural bent of humankind, apart from divine help, seems to be polluted with a self-centeredness that is self-protective, self-absorbed, but even worse, selfish at the expense of others. The human DNA possesses a stubborn persistence toward self-focused living, which is unlike God's original intention for us. Doing what Jesus would do or think or say is not our natural bent. So, apart from God's help to reconfigure that DNA, change is pretty difficult—and in some ways, impossible.

Learned Behavior: From childhood, we are being shaped by our environment and those in it. People of influence in our lives serve as models to us. The ways they relate to us and the ways they relate to others become the molds that shape how we think, process, and relate to ourselves, God, and others. Years into our marriages, we discover that the cultures in which we grew up have as much to do with the ways we function in a marriage and family as any other factor. *We learn much of our behavior.*

Disassociation: How often we hear some great advice from a sermon, read some wisdom in a book, or catch a new idea from one of TV's relationship gurus, and then automatically think of somebody else who needs to hear and apply it! Something inside inclines us to judge or criticize others for that which is our very own shortcoming.

Isn't it amazing how we overlook our own faults and project them onto someone else? We may hear or read some great truth of God that relates to everyday living, but we somehow disassociate it from ourselves and assume that the other guy is the one who really needs it.

With all of these things, and more, going against us, how are we to ever consistently walk our spiritual talk?

THE PATHWAY

Reversal of the above-mentioned barriers would be a good start. Transformation of our human nature would be a huge help. We could unlearn some of our old behaviors and relearn new ways of living. And we could learn to identify our own sins and errors and take responsibility for how we apply our faith to daily living.

The Bible has an action word that best describes the pathway to spiritual integrity: *repent.*

Sounds like a word used by a heavy-breathing TV evangelist, doesn't it? Actually, the meaning and practice of repentance is the pathway God uses to transform our lives. Repentance is the solution to closing the gap between what we say and what we do.

After Jesus was resurrected from the Cross, the tomb, and death, and after being seen by many individuals and groups of people, He was preparing for that incredible "liftoff" back to heaven. Luke records Jesus as saying, "The Christ will suffer and rise from the dead on the third day, and *repentance and forgiveness* of sins will be preached to all nations, beginning at Jerusalem" (24:46-47, emphasis added).

Repentance includes three dynamic steps in the process of transformation. First is the practice of *review and evaluation.* We dare to look back on our life and identify the errors of our way. We confess the same, and truly regret our sins and failures.

Next, we ask God to help us experience a *determination to change.* We need to review what internal beliefs, perspectives, and attitudes have contributed to our waywardness, and commit to change. Third, we *take action leading to change.*

We commonly refer to significant change with the word *transformation*. That's what we need, a renovation from the inside-out that results in real change. How does that happen?

In one sense, a transforming power must come from *outside* ourselves. Such motivation could be some life experience that stimulates change. Or it could be the counsel or impact of others on our lives. Ultimately, it needs to be the direct influence of God's Spirit. A theological term for this is *sanctification*.

However, there also needs to be something from *within* ourselves that contributes to transformation. There are long-held theological views that no good thing resides in the human being that is untransformed by God. Regardless of one's view of the natural human condition, we must still respect the fact the even before Christ enters our lives, we are creations of God and possess capacity for Him. We are spiritual beings. As such, God expects us to cooperate with His work in our lives.

Ephesians 4:22-23 is a terrific expression of the meaning of repentance that leads to transformation. "You were taught, with regard to your former way of life, to put off your old self, which is being corrupted by its deceitful desires."

Captured in those verses are the major ingredients of repentance and transformation: Get a grip on the way you have been living. Figure out what is corrupted and discern your motives. Determine that this "old self" does not match the calling of God on your life. The action of "putting off" is a strong term for intentional and assertive action. It includes the need for courage and discipline.

Next, be made new in the attitude of your mind. Now, this sounds like we need help. It does not say to *make yourself* new, but *be made* new. We need a whole new perspective and way of thinking about ourselves, God, and how we are living. This is in line with Romans 12:2, "Be transformed by the renewing of your mind."

Finally, Paul says, "Put on the new self, created to be like God in true righteousness and holiness" (Ephesians 4:24). Once again, the idea of disciplined and intentional action comes through this verse. Do something that demonstrates the new way of living!

God helping us, we *can* change and *be* changed. We can live the faith we proclaim! Getting there is neither automatic nor easy, but possible and essential. That is the meaning of authentic Christianity—a life lived with integrity. Our beliefs and values guide and shape our attitudes and behaviors. That describes a life of holiness. Our model is Jesus Christ. Becoming like Christ leads us to wholeness and holiness.

We are created to do good. We are saved by faith. We cannot save ourselves, otherwise what Christ did is useless. However, once our lives are turned toward God, we must live a God-oriented life. Behavior must be reflective of our beliefs.

So, what about you? Is there a credibility gap in your life? Are your moods, attitudes, words, and behaviors increasingly in line with what Jesus would say and do? Are you increasing in grace, and do you contribute to peace? Do you extend grace to others, especially those closest to you? Are you really much fun to be around? If not, you need a spiritual make-over, the kind only you and God can achieve together.

Life is dynamic. You might have had it pretty well together a few months or years back, but things change, and so do we. I thought that as I aged, there would be no more problem with certain attitudes, thoughts, and reactions. I was wrong. The Christian life is a living, breathing reality. We must quit excusing sin and stupidity and sullenness in our lives. If we don't, then we trash the reputation of Christ, and we make unbelievers of those around us.

Remember the optimism of God and His grace. God and you can generate all the change that is needed in your life. It does not happen by accident. Take fearless inventory of the details of your life, and how you live it. Determine the areas where change is most needed. Consult the Bible and pray for the intervention of God's Holy Spirit on a day-by-day, hour-by-hour basis. He will give you guidance and alert you when you step over the line. Listen, then obey. Life will be sweeter, and you will leave a trail worth following!

Notes:

*Dallas Willard, *The Divine Conspiracy: Rediscovering Our Hidden Life in God* (San Francisco: Harper Collins, 1998), 1-60.

Scripture Cited: Matthew 7:21; Luke 24:46-47; Romans 12:2; Ephesians 4:22-24; James 1:13-15, 19, 26-27; 2:17-18, 20-21; 3:1-12; 4:7-8

About the Author: Dr. Holdren is currently the executive pastor at Cypress Wesleyan Church, Columbus, Ohio. He served for 28 years as a pastor and 8 years in denominational leadership. He and his wife, Marlene, have two daughters and four grandchildren.

TRUTH TO REMEMBER

Kingdom Christians compassionately
meet the needs of others.

13

ACTIVE COMPASSION

BY C. S. COWLES

"Let my heart be broken by the things that break the heart of God." That poignant sentence, written on the flyleaf of Bob Pierce's Bible during a whirlwind evangelistic tour of post-World War II China, was the tiny seed from which has grown the Giant Sequoia of the world's largest nongovernmental relief organization, World Vision. As an example of their global outreach, they already had over 5,000 workers in Southeast Asia when recent history's most destructive tsunami struck in December, 2004. Within hours, their personnel were delivering blankets, clean water, food, and tents to tens of thousands of shocked survivors. They provided direct assistance to over 1 million people in the first 90 days. The money they raised for tsunami relief eventually exceeded $200 million.

The phenomenal growth and benevolent influence of World Vision, however, pales next to the long-range effect of a time-bomb tucked into two tiny verses in Paul's shortest, humblest, least read, and theologically lightest letter: Philemon. It would take 1,700 years for its mind-altering, tradition-shattering, and socially disruptive revelation to explode. But when it did, it would destroy a bedrock social convention that has endured among virtually all peoples in every part of the known world since the dawn of recorded history —what John Wesley described as "that most vile of all human institutions"—slavery. It is the Bible's least-known and yet most compelling story of "active compassion," or more accurately, "transformative compassion."

A DIAMOND IN THE ROUGH

Philemon was one of Paul's converts in the region of Laodicea, now part of Turkey. His young Greek slave, Onesimus, had not only run away, but robbed his Christian master before fleeing. It was true then, as in our own country's dark past, that a captured slave could be beaten or even killed by his master without recrimination. Slaves were regarded as property to be bought and sold, used and abused, whipped and raped, at the whim of the master. Onesimus's situation as a fugitive was desperate. We do not know why he fled to Rome or how he learned that the apostle was in the city, being held "in chains for the gospel" (v. 13). What we do know is that Onesimus sought out Paul. Based on his previous experience with the apostle, who was Philemon's house guest while evangelizing Laodicea, he knew that he would be received warmly.

Not surprisingly, Paul led Onesimus into a saving relationship with Jesus Christ. Onesimus reciprocated by ministering to the apostle's practical needs. In a play on words that is clear in the original language, Paul says of Onesimus, whose name in Greek means "useful," "Formerly he was *useless* to you, but now he has become *useful* both to you and to me" (v. 11, emphasis added). As a believer, Onesimus was now being true to his name: useful. Such a tight relationship developed between the two that Paul speaks of him as "my son" and "my very heart" (vv. 10, 12).

There came a time when Paul realized that if Onesimus was to ever achieve his potential "as a man and as a brother in the Lord" (v. 16), he would need to return to his earthly master—a very scary proposition for Onesimus, to say the least. It was to expedite his return and, hopefully, mediate a genuine reconciliation between master and slave that Paul wrote this heartfelt personal letter. It was to be hand-delivered by Onesimus himself (see Colossians 4:7-9, 16). The apostle's plea is that Philemon will receive his fugitive slave without recrimination.

Yet, something far deeper and more momentous is going on here: Paul wanted Philemon to not only forgive Onesimus but *set him free*. "Perhaps the reason [Onesimus] was separated from you for a little while was that you might have him back for good—no longer as a slave, but better than a slave, as a dear brother" (vv. 15-16).

No longer a slave! By those four words, Paul said something that not only transformed Onesimus's status in ways that would impact the Church for all future generations, but unleashed a liberating force that would one day upset the hierarchy of social relations in ways never before imagined. By those four words, Paul launched history's first abolition movement. And there would be no turning back.

STRIKING THE CHAINS

There are two kinds of compassion, both on display in this letter. Because of his rash action, Onesimus had placed himself in serious jeopardy. He desperately needed help, the kind of immediate hands-on "active compassion" commended by Jesus in His parable of the sheep and the goats: feeding the hungry, giving drink to the thirsty, caring for the homeless, clothing the naked, healing the sick, and ministering to those "in prison" (see Matthew 25:31-46).

There is, however, a more profound kind of "active compassion": it is to confront those systems of societal and institutionalized structures of evil that impoverish, enslave, and ultimately destroy human beings. Jesus came not only to "preach the gospel to the poor" but to *"proclaim release to the captives"* (Luke 4:18, NASB, emphasis added). To minister to those in prison, as Wesley and the early Methodists did every week, was one thing. To tear down prison walls and set the captives free was a vastly more challenging enterprise.

Yet, that was precisely Paul's intention: he wanted Philemon to *strike the chains* that had Onesimus bound so that he could return and continue his personal ministry to the apostle in Rome. More importantly, he saw in Onesimus great potential for ministry that could be realized only if he were a free man. What was his rationale for such an unprecedented and scandalously radical request? It can be framed in the form of a rhetorical question: *How can any person, much less a Christian, keep a "brother" in chains?*

What Paul was asking Philemon to do not only went against the grain of deeply rooted social convention but was patently "unscriptural." As early as the days of Noah, we read: "Cursed be Canaan! The lowest of slaves will he be to his brothers" (Genesis 9:25). The ancient Israelites, who were once slaves themselves, owned slaves. While the Mosaic Law forbade enslaving fellow Israelites, it not only permitted, but encouraged them to buy slaves from other nations, who would then become their property (see Leviticus 25:42-46). In both the testaments, slavery as a legitimate social institution is presumed. Paul himself accommodated the gospel to the temper of the times by counseling slaves to be obedient to their masters and masters to treat their slaves kindly (see Ephesians 6:5-9).

Thus, it is not surprising that the Old School Presbyterian General Assembly report of 1845 would reaffirm, in the face of the growing abolition movement, that slavery was based on "some of the plainest declarations of the Word of God." The *Princeton Review* was even more strident: "The history of [biblical] interpretation furnishes no examples of more willful and violent perversions of the sacred text than are to be found in the writings of the abolitionists."[1] In a widely distributed 1837 article, "Slavery as a Positive Good," John C. Calhoun protested against anti-slave agitators:

But *I take higher ground.* I hold that in the present

state of civilization, where two races of different origin, and distinguished by color, and other physical differences, as well as intellectual, are brought together, the relation now existing in the slaveholding States between the two, is, instead of an evil, a good—a positive good. ...I hold then, that there never has yet existed a wealthy and civilized society in which one portion of the community did not, in point of fact, live on the labor of the other. Broad and general as is this assertion, it is fully borne out by history (emphasis added).[2]

It is against the background of these bedrock assumptions that we can better appreciate the radicality of Paul's letter to Philemon. Rather than directly challenge slavery—which given the embryonic state of the Church at that time would have been a futile gesture—he laid an ax to the demeaning, depersonalizing, and dehumanizing tap root that supported the whole despicable enterprise. Unlike the framers of our Constitution who counted slaves as "three-fifths" persons, Paul esteemed Onesimus as a "five-fifths" (that is, complete) human being, wondrously created by God, and now a "son of God" by faith in Christ (see John 1:12; 1 John 3:1-2). More than that, Paul declared that Onesimus was to be regarded no longer as property, but as "a dear brother" (v. 16) on equal footing with Philemon and Paul himself.

Thus in one bold stroke, Paul not only countered the clear teaching of the Old Testament but confronted, challenged, and abolished all artificial distinctions of "origins," "color," and "other differences" (Calhoun) that master races had for so long used to rationalize their subjugation of supposedly "inferior" races and social classes of people. Never before had anyone dared to proclaim, as Paul does in his letter to the Galatians, that, "There is neither Jew nor Greek, *slave nor free*, male nor female, for you are all one in Christ Jesus" (3:28, emphasis added).

Though it would take many centuries for Christians to

understand the full scope of this "freedom [for which] Christ has set us free" (Galatians 5:1), when that truth finally burst upon human consciousness, it would bring about a sea-change in the way people would look at slaves. We see this eloquently expressed in the preamble of the Constitution of the Oberlin Anti-Slavery Society formed in 1835, to which two of my great-great uncles, John and Henry Cowles, fixed their signatures:

> [The slave] is constituted by God a moral agent, the keeper of his own happiness, the executive of his own powers, the accountable arbiter of his own choice; personal ownership his birthright, unforfeited and invaluable; liberty, and the pursuit of happiness his chartered rights, inherited from his maker and guaranteed by all the laws of his being. . . . [He] is immortal, created in God's image, the purchase of a Savior's blood, visited by the Holy Ghost, and united to a citizenship with angels and to fellowship with God.[3]

TWELVE MEN WHO CHANGED THE WORLD

Who could have imagined that a handful of humble Quakers and evangelical Anglicans, meeting amid the clutter and acrid smells of a small print shop in the bosom of London's business district on May 22, 1787, would launch a movement that would create massive social and economic upheaval throughout the British Empire, incite the bloodiest war in America's history, and forever change the landscape of human relationships?[4] In order to better appreciate the radicality of their achievement, we must consider the enormity of the challenges those early anti-slave reformers faced.

First, *it was a world of bondage.* Whether serfs or slaves, the overwhelming majority of people were virtual prisoners. They labored with little or no remuneration, worked from sunup to sundown—sometimes chained together—and were often subjected to cruel whippings. One historian remarked that "the peculiar institution" of the 18th century was not slavery, but freedom.

Second, *it was a world dependent upon slavery*. "What a glorious and advantageous trade this is," wrote a British slave merchant. "It is the hinge on which all the trade of this globe moves."[5] The path to riches was built on the bruised, bent, and bloodied backs of slaves. Vast New World sugar, cotton, and coffee plantations worked by African slaves, not only made fortunes for their owners, but contributed significantly to Great Britain's rise as the superpower of its day. The Anglican Church, Oxford University, several missionary organizations, and a wide assortment of philanthropies directly benefited from the produce of Caribbean plantations. To supply the human raw materials needed to work the plantations, British ships alone transported 11,000,000 African slaves to their New World colonies between 1555 and 1795, with 1,400,000 perishing en route.

Third, *it was a world of unspeakable cruelty*. If hapless African captives should survive the brutal march to the coast, bound together by their necks in wooden yokes, and then the agonies of the perilous Atlantic crossing, they would be worked to an early death, all the while subjected to cruel punishments. It is doubtful that there is any passage in Scripture that has caused more torturous pain to greater numbers of people over a longer period of time than this: "If a man beats his male or female slave with a rod and the slave dies as a direct result, he must be punished, but he is not to be punished if the slave gets up after a day or two, since the slave is his property" (Exodus 21:20-21). Frederick Douglass, the ex-slave who became one of America's most eloquent and fervent abolitionists, tells of a Christian master who regularly whipped his slaves, whether they had done anything reprehensible or not, just to remind them who was boss.

When James Stephen, an idealistic young English attorney, fled to Barbados to escape his romantic scandals, he was shocked to witness a trial in which two slaves, falsely accused of killing a white man, were executed by being slowly roasted alive. From 6:30 to 9:30 each night, he could hear the pitiful cries of plantation slaves being whipped. He watched two slave women carry a third out into the rain, where they picked maggots out of festering wounds received in a whipping five days earlier. What he experienced there would turn him into a fervent abolitionist.

Finally, *it was a world accustomed to the inhumanity of slavery.* Even John Newton, slave ship captain and composer of one of the world's most popular songs, "Amazing Grace," failed to see any contradiction between his new life in Christ and his lucrative "calling." Newton's diary is replete with descriptions of rapturous prayer times while pacing the deck of his ship, totally oblivious to the agonizing wails of injured, sick, and dying slaves chained to their wooden pallets directly under his feet. It would be 30 years before he, too, would acknowledge the evils of slavery. The great 18th-century revivalist, George Whitfield, purchased a plantation in Georgia along with its 50 slaves. When criticized for not setting his slaves free, he wrote a fiery tract defending slavery as a "God-ordained institution." Such was the spiritual blindness of the times.

AN "ACTIVE COMPASSION" MOVEMENT TAKES SHAPE

What John and Charles Wesley were to the Great Evangelical Awakening that swept England earlier, Thomas Clarkson was to the anti-slavery movement. Already a distinguished Cambridge University scholar at 26, and a head taller than most Englishmen, he cut an impressive figure wherever he went. Thanks to the Wesleyan revivals that had raised concern for the poor, disadvantaged, and oppressed to hitherto unknown levels, and also an avalanche of books, pamphlets, and articles describing the horrors of slavery, some authored by ex-slaves, Clarkson and his colleagues

were able to capitalize on a rising tide of anti-slavery senti-
ment among the general populace.

For the next half-century, Clarkson traveled the length
and breadth of the British Empire, speaking to gatherings
small and large, organizing cells of anti-slavery activists in
virtually every town and city, leading boycotts on slave-
grown produce (over 300,000 refused to buy Caribbean sugar in one campaign alone), and submitting huge stacks of
signed petitions to parliament again and again. He and others innovated many of the techniques of swaying popular
opinion that have been utilized by social and political action
groups ever since.

The abolitionists found a powerful ally in parliament,
William Wilberforce (1759-1833). Born into a family of
wealth and social standing, and having been largely raised by
an aunt who was a staunch Methodist, he underwent a deep
spiritual conversion at 26 years of age. He thenceforth devoted his enormous energies to social reforms, especially
ending the slave trade which he considered to be a moral rot
eating away at the British Empire's soul. After years of persistent effort, the House of Commons passed a law banning
the capture, transportation, and sale of African slaves in
1792. For the first time ever, at least one reprehensible aspect
of slavery had been declared illegal.

Wilberforce and the abolition activists had long believed that if the slave trade could be abolished, slavery itself
would soon wither away. They were wrong. Unable to pur-
chase new slaves, plantation owners simply began an aggres-
sive program of breeding their own. So Wilberforce and the
anti-slave activists redirected their energies toward emancipation. That proved to be a more challenging process. It
would be nearly 40 more long years before Wilberforce
would receive, on his deathbed in 1833, the news that the
House of Commons had enacted legislation setting slaves
free throughout the British Empire. Of the original 12 activists, only Clarkson was still alive to see slavery ended.

Abraham Lincoln's Emancipation Proclamation followed 30 years later. By the end of the 19th century, slavery as a social institution had been abolished virtually around the world.[6] "Never doubt," said Margaret Mead, "that a small group of thoughtful, committed citizens can change the world. Indeed, it is the only thing that ever has."[7]

PHILEMON'S HISTORIC LEGACY

What happened to Onesimus? From the letters of Ignatius written in A.D. 110, we learn that Onesimus not only had been given his bill of freedom but had risen to become the bishop of the Church at Ephesus. By that time, Ephesus had become the dynamic center of the rapidly growing Christian movement. It was also a critical period when the Church was being torn apart by the Gnostic heresy within and suffering increasing Roman persecution without. Who would have been in a better position to hold the Church steady during this time of difficult challenges than Onesimus, one of the aging apostle's brightest disciples? It can be said, with considerable justification, that *in the beginning, Paul saved Onesimus, but in the end Onesimus saved Paul's churches.*

We also discover that Onesimus was the first to gather copies of Paul's scattered letters into one corpus. When we see the strategic role Onesimus played in preserving Paul's writings, a larger picture can be seen. *In the beginning, Paul set Onesimus free for ministry; in the end, Onesimus set Paul free for the ages!*

We can never tell, when devoting ourselves to the noble calling of "active compassion," what chains might be struck and what energies released!

Notes:

1. *The Princeton Review*, vol. 10, Issue 4 (October 1838), 603-04.

2. <http://www.assumption.edu/ahc/Kansas/abolition/abolition.html>

3. <http://www.oberlin.edu/external/EOG/Documents/Oberlin AntiSlaveryCon.htm>.

4. This story is told in fascinating detail in Adam Hochschild's, *Bury the Chains* (New York: Houghton Mifflin Co., 2005).

5. Hochschild, 14.

6. Online *Encyclopedia Britannia*, <http:/www.britannia.com/bios/Wilberforce.html>.

7. Cited by Hochschild in *Bury the Chains*, 7.

Scripture Cited: Genesis 9:25; Exodus 21:20-21; Luke 4:18; Galatians 3:28; 5:1; Philemon 10-13, 15-16

About the Author: Dr. Cowles is professor of religion and philosophy at Point Loma Nazarene University, and professor emeritus of Northwest Nazarene University.